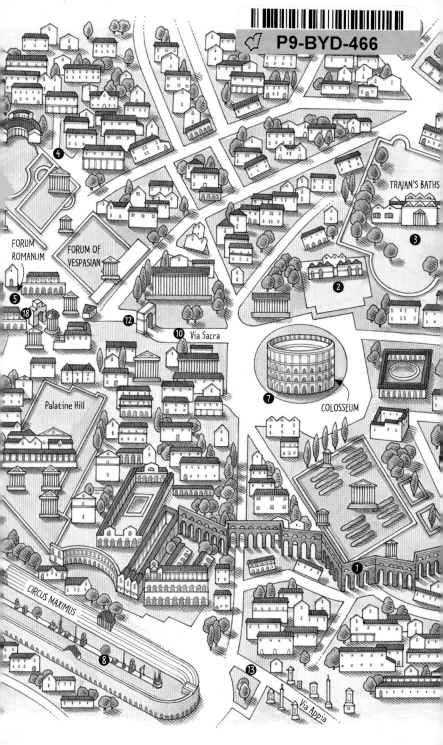

P9-BYD-466

TRAJAN'S BATHS

③

FORUM
ROMANUM

FORUM OF
VESPASIAN

⑤

⑱

⑫

②

⑩ Via Sacra

COLOSSEUM

⑦

Palatine Hill

①

CIRCUS MAXIMUS

⑧

⑬

Via Appia

Dear reader,

This book is based on my adventures in Ancient Rome. I must have made hundreds of trips back in time, but I still remember the tingling excitement of my very first visit.

On my travels, I took pages and pages of notes. Two friends of mine — Lesley Sims and Louie Stowell — kindly helped me turn these scribbled thoughts into a book. Hope you enjoy it.

All the best,

Lucius Minimus Britanicus*

* As you might have guessed, this isn't my real name, it's just what I call myself when I'm in Rome. When I visit other times and other places, I go by other names. But that's another story. Or stories, I suppose...

A Visitor's Guide to

Ancient ROME

Based on the travels of
Lucius Minimus Britanicus

Compiled by Lesley Sims and Louie Stowell

Illustrated by Christyan Fox, Ian Jackson,
Ian McNee, John Woodcock and Peter Allen

Designed by Marc Maynard
and Nayera Everall

This is the Senate – the place where Rome's rulers meet.

Assassin

Wealthy politicians known as senators

Rome's ruler, the emperor

Senator giving a speech

Contents

Internet links

If you're not up to taking an actual trip to Ancient Rome, why not take a virtual tour instead? Go to www.usborne-quicklinks.com and type the keywords "guide to ancient rome".

There you'll find links to websites with virtual tours and reconstructions of Ancient Rome. The links are regularly reviewed and updated, but please note, Usborne Publishing is not responsible for the availability or content of websites other than its own. Please follow the internet safety guidelines displayed on the Usborne Quicklinks Website.

A note about dates:

Since this book is about ancient times, it includes some odd-looking dates. Dates that say BC after them are the oldest. BC stands for "Before Christ", and the dates are counted as the number of years before the date that historians used to think was Jesus's birthday.

Dates without letters refer to the "modern" era.

Confused? Better get used to it. You are about to embark on a time travel adventure, after all, so you'll be having all kinds of strange, new, mind-boggling experiences.

Part one:

The basics

Time travel always goes more smoothly when you know what you're letting yourself in for. I say this from experience. My first visit to Ancient Rome was brilliant - don't get me wrong - but I wish I'd been much better prepared.

For example, when I went to the "Games" in Rome, I was expecting light-hearted fun. What I got was the most horrifically violent spectacle imaginable. I still have nightmares.

That's why I want to pass on my tips to other time tourists like you, so you know what to expect. Let's start with the basics...

Exploring the backstreets of Rome will give your nose some serious exercise.

First impressions

When I arrived in Ancient Rome - around 2,000 years ago, if you're counting from the 21st century - the first thing I noticed was the smell, as my nostrils filled with a a mix of cooking smells and some less pleasant whiffs. Rome is pretty clean for its time, but parts of it are still ankle deep in muck.

It's a beautiful city, though, full of statues, fountains, and shiny marble buildings. Many of these are temples, as the Romans were a god-fearing lot - with dozens of gods to fear.

Rome's about halfway down the map of Italy.

Rome is built on seven hills. But they're very gentle, so you won't be spending your trip panting for breath.

In the beginning

Rome wasn't always so fancy. About 3,000 years ago, it was just a few groups of scruffy huts on the hills around the River Tiber. Over time, these villages merged and became the city of Rome. The people who lived there came to be known as the Romans. So far, so simple. But the earliest days of Rome remain a mystery. Here's the most famous (probably untrue) story of how Rome began.

8

A not-so-big-bad wolf

Once upon a time, there were two princes named Romulus and Remus. As babies, these twin brothers were chucked in the River Tiber by their wicked uncle.

Luckily, they were washed ashore and looked after by a she-wolf. I wonder how they learned to talk? Or did they just growl?

These would-be wolf-cubs grew up big and strong and, before too long, they went back to kill their unpleasant uncle.

This picture shows a statue of Romulus, Remus and their "mother".

The evil twin wins

After killing their uncle, the brothers built a city exactly where the wolf found them. But during the opening ceremony, Remus made fun of his brother... so Romulus killed him. Then he named the city after himself – Rome. If Romulus had lost the fight, maybe this book would be about "Reme"?

Top tips for tourists

No. 1: Just say no to kings

The Romans really, really hate kings. They used to have them, but their kings behaved badly and were booted out.

So, if you happen to think having a king or queen is quite a nice idea really, keep it to yourself – or risk being very unpopular in Rome.

The Senate

In the beginning, Rome had kings, but later, a group of men called the Senate made the big decisions. In time, they grew less powerful, but they still had a very high opinion of themselves.

This coin shows the Senate House, where Senators met.

66 *Want to hear about Rome from people who've lived there all their lives? Look for scrolls like this one. They contain quotes from locals as well as from super-famous Roman authors (ok, famous in Rome, anyway.)* **99**

When to go?

So, which year should you visit Rome? It's a tricky question. Go back too far - say, to the year 750BC, when Rome was supposedly founded - all you'd see would be a few rickety huts and some sheep. But, pick the wrong date later on and you could end up slap bang in the middle of a war.

I recommend 118 as a good year. Rome was at its most bustling, noisy and exciting then - but not exciting in the "being attacked by hairy barbarians" sense.

At that time, the ruler of Rome was known as an emperor - sort of a cross between a king and an army general. Roman emperors liked nothing better than conquering foreigners and, over time, they gobbled up most of Europe (and beyond) into what's known as the Roman Empire.

What's this map?

This map shows the Roman Empire in 118, when it was the biggest it would ever be. Rome itself is the red dot in the middle.

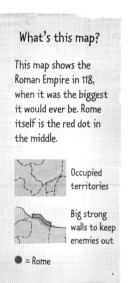

Occupied territories

Big strong walls to keep enemies out

● = Rome

The Roman Empire in the year 118

Atlantic Ocean

Black Sea

Mediterranean Sea

Aegean Sea

More than just a city

You won't just be visiting a city: in the year 118, Rome is the most important place in the world. (At least, the Romans think so.) It's where the emperor, Hadrian, lives, plus almost a million other people. Given that, you'll probably be relieved to hear that the Romans have already invented a decent sewer system.

Trend-setting Emperor Hadrian was the first emperor to grow a beard. Soon, hairy chins were all the rage.

Fitting in

If you see statues of a man with a beard, it's probably Emperor Hadrian. And if anyone asks, you're a big fan - sucking up to the emperor is a very Roman thing to do, so it'll help you fit right in.

Mind you, they'd probably be asking in Latin - Rome's official language - so you might just have to nod, smile and pretend you understand. (There are some handy phrases at the back of this book if you want to try your hand at talking like the locals.)

When you visit, you won't need a visa, or even a passport. Rome's open to everyone. As long as you show respect to the emperor (and his soldiers) and don't go around saying you're from the future, you'll be fine.

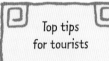

Top tips for tourists

No. 2: Handy Latin

Even if you don't learn much Latin, there's one phrase that'll help you get loads of perks: "Civis Romanus sum" – say Key-wiss Row (as in boat) mar-nuss sum. It means, "I'm a Roman citizen." Roman citizens get treated better than anyone else. Unfair? Sure, but you might as well benefit.

Who lives in Rome?

Romans, right? Well, yes and no. Lots of the people there aren't citizens (or *cives*, in Latin) of Rome, which means they aren't "proper" Romans. I bet they wish they were, though.

Citizens get all the good stuff. For example, they can vote in elections but they pay less in tax than non-citizens. Oh, and they can't be whipped, tortured, or executed in nasty ways.

From poshos to plebs

But not all citizens get the same perks. A Roman's lot in life depends on which class they're born into and what sex they are. To get the best treatment, pretend to be a patrician. And - if you're female - a man.

Patricians: the richest, poshest Romans. The top of the social tree.

Equites: the businessmen and bankers. Not top dogs, but wealthy.

Plebeians: the poorest. But at least they're still citizens.

Non-citizens

Romans look down on non-citizens. If you're pretending to be a citizen (recommended), you should look down on this lot:

Provincials: people who live in the Empire and pay tax

Foreigners: everyone who lives outside the Empire

Slaves: owned by others and bought and sold like property

Top jobs and awful ones

You definitely don't want to get mistaken for a slave. Most slaves lead awful lives. They have to work like, well, slaves. They don't get paid, and they often get beaten – or even executed.

If slaves are at the bottom of the heap, who's at the top? That'd be the consuls who are a little like modern prime ministers, only there are two at once. If you're interested in the job, check out what you need to do to get there on the right.

The road to success

If a young man wants to scale the career ladder, he has to:

Step 1: Serve as an army officer.

Step 2: Work as a *quaestor*, a sort of government accountant.

Step 3: Be an *aedile*, responsible for public places and games.

Step 4: Be a *praetor* – a judge in the law courts

Finally, he has a shot at being consul. This rod thing is the consul's symbol.

13

Planning your trip

When you're getting ready to visit Rome, what should you pack? What will the weather be like? What about food?

Weather: Most of the time, Rome has mild weather and the odd rain shower. But I'd avoid visiting in June, July or August when it can be disgustingly hot and sweaty. Most rich Romans leave town in summer, and I think they have the right idea.

Shorts and a t-shirt keep you cool, but might shock the locals. See pages 102-105 for Roman fashion tips.

What to pack: Don't worry about clothes. You'll be able to buy tunics and other Roman clothing from the markets. It's a good idea to head there first, to avoid looking out of place and inviting awkward questions about where you came from.

The water from Rome's fountains is safe, and free of added chemicals too.

Refreshments: There are lots of places to buy snacks. You can't get canned drinks though: they haven't been invented yet. But you won't go thirsty - there are hundreds of fountains dotted around the city. Just take a water bottle to fill up.

14

Getting your bearings

All packed? Toothbrush? Sunscreen? Good. You're almost ready for Rome. But first, here are a few tips to help you prepare yourself mentally for your arrival in Rome in the year 118:

1) It will be busy, noisy, smelly and smoky. Brace yourself!

2) There are no cars or public transport, so be prepared to walk everywhere.

3) Everyone will be speaking Latin. Check out the phrases on page 118.

4) Try not to act shocked by people whipping their slaves. Remember, you're a Roman. Slavery is as normal as breathing.

Pocket money

There's information about Roman money at the back of the book.

But, unless you happen to be an ancient coin collector, how are you going to get money?

Easy. Just take some pepper with you from your kitchen cupboard, or any old cooking spices. You'll be able to trade these for hard cash, as they're worth a lot of money in Ancient Rome.

The fast moving city

The Romans are never satisfied with their city and Rome can sometimes feel like one big building site. Emperors build new buildings as often as other people blow their noses. This means Rome's always changing, so some of the things you read about may be different by the time you arrive.

If you spot a building that's not in this guide, don't worry. It was probably built since I visited.

Where to stay

Picture yourself in a lavish hotel room, with fluffy pillows and a steaming shower.

Now forget that, because there aren't any five star hotels in Rome – well, only one, and that's for famous foreign leaders. There aren't really any tourist hotels, and most Roman accomodation would probably get minus-stars in a modern guidebook. But if you follow these tips, you should at least find somewhere that isn't a health hazard and, with luck, you'll find somewhere cosy.

Renting

With no hotels around, I imagine you'll be renting. If you haven't managed to scrape together much Roman cash, an apartment in an *insula* (block) will be cheapest. A *domus* (town house) would be comfier but they're very expensive and there aren't many of them.

Key to the plan below

❶ Garden

❷ Dining room

❸ Kitchen

❹ Storerooms

❺ Baker's shop

❻ Street

❼ Shop selling trinkets

❽ Storeroom

❾ Ladies' sitting room

❿ Study

⓫ Atrium (central courtyard)

This is a plan of a town house, showing the ground floor. Bedrooms are on the second floor.

The top floors can be very rickety, and even collapse. If you hear creaking, get out immediately.

Avoid places above taverns, or you'll be woken up every time someone bursts into drunken song – or a drunken fight.

Steer clear of bigger appartment blocks if you value your sleep – and your life. Rent in Rome is sky-high and families often rent out rooms for extra cash. Big blocks can end up very crowded, making them death-traps if a fire breaks out.

Also, with so many people packed together, and no sound-proofing, you might end up getting to know the people next door better than you'd like.

Why not rent the apartment of an out-of-town government official? You might even get the household staff included in the rent.

Top tips for tourists

No. 4: Nightly noise

Avoid places near markets, or the noise of carts being unloaded will keep you awake.

In Rome, rush-hour is at night. Most wheeled vehicles are only allowed to enter the city between sunset and sunrise, to avoid traffic jams during business hours.

Top tips for tourists

No. 5: Air freshener

Before you agree to rent anywhere, check that the landlord, or his agent, arranges for the stairs and hallways to be swept and cleaned regularly.

Your rooms will still get stuffy, though. Pliny (a Roman writer and senator) burns bread in his rooms to mask the smell. Only try it if you prefer the smell of charred toast to sweat.

No mod cons

If you're very lucky, you can get an apartment with running water, a bathroom and a kitchen. But most apartments are very basic, just somewhere to crash, with no luxury touches. Even the fanciest places don't have glass in their windows.

You'll have a much better time if you grit your teeth and don't expect too much. On the plus side, you can have a nice bath (more on that later) at the public baths, and there are plenty of cheap places to buy ready-made meals. Who wants to waste valuable time-travel time cooking, anyway?

Where's the bathroom?

If you need the lavatory when you're at home in Rome, I've got bad news. There probably won't be one if you're in cheap accommodation. But don't panic, you won't have to use a bucket. Most Romans use public lavatories. These don't have cubicles, but why feel shy? Romans don't.

They see going for a pee as a chance for a nice chat. But remember your wallet as there's a fee of one *as*. (Check out page 114-115 for more info on Roman coins.)

In spite of the smell, lavatories are clean, thanks to a constant flow of water.

18

Stinking sewers

Drainage systems are probably the world's most boring conversation topic. But you wouldn't enjoy the kind of "interesting" that you'd get in a big city without drains. Let's hear it for Rome's super-duper sewage system.

Underground sewers wash waste into the Tiber river via the massive underground Cloaca Maxima - or "Great Drain" in English.

The Romans are very proud of their achievements in sewage technology, although parts of the city are still rather ripe by modern standards.

Waste is meant to be poured into the sewer but some lazy types chuck it out the window.

Clean water is carried into Rome along stone channels called aqueducts.

Waterworks

The Romans are just as good at providing clean water as they are at sluicing away filth.

There are ten great channels, or aqueducts, which carry fresh water into Rome.

These feed all the city's baths, fountains and lavatories.

Rome's plumbers are truly some of the best in the (ancient) world.

All you can eat

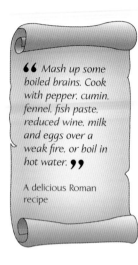

66 *Mash up some boiled brains. Cook with pepper, cumin, fennel, fish paste, reduced wine, milk and eggs over a weak fire, or boil in hot water.* 99

A delicious Roman recipe

You won't go hungry in Rome. Wherever you turn, someone will be trying to sell you food. Want a hot meal? A snack? A dish made from a peculiar part of an animal? The city's full of rowdy taverns and bustling market stalls to choose from.

If you visit a tavern, you might find graffiti on the walls - in Latin. But I wouldn't repeat what you read, in case you're telling someone their father's a smelly goat - some of it's very insulting.

It's perfectly polite to eat with your fingers, but many Romans carry a knife and spoon around. (They don't use forks.)

There aren't any microwaves. Food is kept warm in jars at the counter.

Snack bars

Many people eat on the go, though most snack bars have somewhere you can sit down. Burgers and fries haven't been invented but other fast food is very popular. Even the pickiest eater should be able to find something they like, from bread and cheese to hot pies, sausages, bacon and beans, or fried fish.

Food poisoning is pretty common though, so if a snack bar looks dirty, back away fast if you value your guts.

If your Latin isn't much good, never fear. Snack bars display pictures of the food they serve, so you won't order fried cow's udders by mistake.

Rich food, poor food

A wealthy Roman might start the day with a snack of bread or wheat biscuits dipped in honey, then lunch on bread and cheese or some salad, eggs and cold meat. Dinner tends to be the blow-out meal of the day.

Poor people have a duller diet. Day after day, it's bread, porridge and the odd bowl of stew. One bonus is the free grain that the emperor hands out. It's not just because he's nice. If the poor get too hungry, they might start riots, and free grain is cheaper than clearing up after an angry mob.

Healthy eating

If you avoid food poisoning, you can eat very healthily.

There's a wide variety of salad and veg, plus all kinds of fresh fruit – from melons and figs to plums and pears, all locally grown. Romans don't use chemicals on their crops so everything's organic.

21

Making *garum* (fish sauce) can be a disgusting process, but Romans think the sauce itself is delicious. I'd take their word for it.

Spicing things up

Chefs in Rome tend to be heavy-handed with the herbs and spices, and douse most dishes in rich, gloopy sauces.

Some suspicious souls might think this is to disguise the fact that you're actually eating rat meat. I wouldn't say that to a Roman chef, though. In my experience, it's best to be polite to anyone with a big knife and the opportunity to spit in your food.

One extra-explosive taste sensation is a salty fish sauce known as *garum*, made from fish guts left to rot in brine for six weeks. It's the Roman version of ketchup, but I'm not sure I'd put it on my burger.

Drink up

You can buy grape juice or honey-sweetened water from street vendors. There are also dozens of elaborate stone drinking fountains in the city, like the one in the picture on the right.

Wine is on sale everywhere, but it's not like the modern stuff. It often comes spiced or sweetened with honey and is generally watered down.

No clue why this man has an eagle on his head. But the water tastes nice.

Sweet treats

Sugar has to be shipped all the way from India, so it's not used in cooking. But there are a wide variety of delicious honey-sweetened delicacies on offer. I recommend trying a sticky honeycake or a freshly baked, flaky pastry. (Now I've made myself hungry.)

Daily bread

Like bread? You'll love Roman food. Bread is eaten at every meal, and the city's bakers make loaves in all shapes and sizes - often with added seeds, nuts, herbs and spices.

Unfortunately, there's another hidden ingredient: grit. All ancient flour contains tiny pieces of stone, from the grinding process. This can be tough on the teeth, though it usually won't do too much damage. Still, chew with care.

If you'd rather prepare your own food, many bakeries will heat food you've made in their ovens for a small fee - the Roman answer to the microwave.

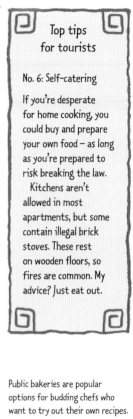

Top tips for tourists

No. 6: Self-catering

If you're desperate for home cooking, you could buy and prepare your own food – as long as you're prepared to risk breaking the law.

Kitchens aren't allowed in most apartments, but some contain illegal brick stoves. These rest on wooden floors, so fires are common. My advice? Just eat out.

Public bakeries are popular options for budding chefs who want to try out their own recipes.

Feasting fit to bust

Top tips
for tourists

No. 7: Gate-crashing

To get a feast invite,
try pretending to be an
important person from
a distant part of the
Empire. By the time they
can send a messenger to
check out your story,
you'll be long gone. To
seem more convincing,
rope in friends to
pretend to be your
slaves, or hire real ones.

To dine with Romans, you'll need two
things: 1) patience and 2) a large stomach.
The evening meal, known as *cena*, begins
in the afternoon, but can last for hours – all
night, if the host really wants to show off.

Not all Romans gorge themselves on
lavish banquets – most eat simple dinners
of roast poultry or fish with vegetables.

But when a rich Roman puts on a
feast, it's something else. If you want
to experience a truly eye-popping, gut-
boggling extravaganza, try to wangle
yourself an invite to one at some point.

You might get to try
flamingo tongues
or sow's udders
and sea urchins.

Dig in with your fingers. Slaves
will wipe your hands whenever
you want.

Slaves wait on diners. This may
feel really weird, but it's all
part of the authentic Roman
experience.

Waited on hand and foot

Don't take it personally if a slave rushes over to wash your feet when you arrive. It's not that they're pongy, it's just something everyone has to do before they enter the dining room. When you've been shown to your seat, a slave will wash your hands too. It's time to lie back and relax. The only thing you'll have to do for yourself is chew.

Acrobats and musicians are usually on hand to amuse diners.

When I say lie back, I mean that literally. Guests recline on bed-like couches to eat. If you want to act like a well-to-do Roman, think of chairs as below your dignity, only for little kids and slaves. Chairs, pah!

Only the best

You might find yourself eating off very fancy plates at a feast. It's your host's way of showing off how rich he is. So take the hint and praise his tableware.

"These silver dishes are splendid!"

"What's this for? Straining the sauce? Fab!"

"What a lovely cup!"

"Where did you get this gorgeous bowl?"

25

Finger food

Tiny spoons are often provided for the egg and shellfish starters. But most people just dig in with their fingers.

This gets messy, so slaves pour perfumed water over your hands and wipe them dry between courses.

Table manners... ?

What table manners? Your fellow diners won't have any, at least not by most modern standards. Not only do they spit, they also show how much they're enjoying their meal by letting out big fat burps.

In fact, the host might get offended if you don't burp at all. He might think you don't appreciate his food. Perhaps this isn't a habit to take home with you, but there's an old expression, "When in Rome, do as the Romans do." So you'd better do it.

Table talk

Flattery always goes down well as a way to break the ice. If your host has a tablecloth, why not compliment him on that? Tablecloths are the latest fad, and anyone who's anyone will probably have one.

On the whole, people tend to gossip rather than talk about serious stuff. But if the talk gets political, definitely don't insult the emperor. He might hear about it, which could make the rest of your stay less than pleasant. If your Latin's anything like mine, you might prefer to keep quiet and just enjoy the musicians and dancers.

If you're unlucky, the host might read you his poetry.

On the menu

Arrive hungry: seven courses are the norm, beginning with simple cold dishes. After a sip of honey wine, the menu can get exotic. Things you'd usually see in a zoo or a pet store could appear on your plate. But if you don't like a course, there'll be another along shortly.

Roman dishes can look really spectacular. (Unless you're a vegetarian.)

Menu

GUSTATIO (STARTER)
A selection of radishes, lettuce, eggs, mushrooms, oysters, cheese and sardines

ENTRÉES
Stuffed dormice
Fish fed on sewage
Cow's udders served with hot rolls

ROASTS
Roast ostrich with leeks fried in honey
Whole piglet with a herb sauce
served with cabbage, turnips,
beans and peas

SECUNDAE MENSAE (DESSERT)
Honey cakes, stuffed dates, fresh
fruit, including apples, pears
and grapes, figs and nuts

There wouldn't actually be a menu, but a typical Roman feast might include some of the food listed above.

Mystery meat

Some cooks pride themselves on their ability to disguise food, e.g. making pork look like fish or duck.

They also like to use odd parts of animals, or creatures you wouldn't usually think of as food. So, ignorance might be bliss. If you take a bite of a mystery dish, you might prefer not to know you're eating snails fed on raw flesh, for example.

Top tips
for tourists

No. 8: Pick the right door

Most bath houses have three entrances – one for men, one for women, and one for slaves.
    To avoid any embarassment, make sure you use the right one. You don't want people to think you're a slave and start ordering you to help them undress.

Romans love to have a chat while they're bathing. They even do business deals at the baths.

Very public baths

Romans like to take a bath most days. Perhaps you do too. But you probably don't take your friends with you. In Rome, washing is a sociable activity. It's more like going to the swimming pool than soaking in the tub at home.

The public baths (known as *thermae*) are giant leisure complexes – a cross between a luxury swimming pool, a shopping mall and a health spa. Only everyone's naked. Romans aren't exactly shy, are they?

If you can ignore all the naked people, the *thermae* are quite a sight to see, with marble pillars, high, domed ceilings and statues in every corner. But, although they look like art galleries, the baths are noisy, lively places.

There are also some smaller, private baths if you're the quiet type. These exclusive, ultra-luxurious bath houses are usually for the rich, but if you manage to get invited to a feast at a rich Roman's house, why not try pushing your luck a bit further? Ask for an invite to one.

Opening hours

Most public baths open around mid-morning and close at sunset, but you need to check who's allowed in when. Men and women are admitted to the bathing areas at separate times of day - usually women in the morning, and men in the afternoon.

You might have to pay a small fee. But sometimes, rich, important citizens pay everyone's fees for them - usually when they're trying to win an election. (Er, I mean, out of the goodness of their hearts.)

One of these bathers is going to be disappointed.

Soap dodgers

There's no soap in Rome, but the Romans have other ways to get you squeaky clean. The baths will provide plentiful supplies of oil. This is smeared all over your body by slaves, then scraped off - along with the grime - with a curved metal gadget called a *strigil.* This leaves your skin as smooth and soft as a baby's bottom.

Strigils can be rented, but they're cheap to buy from markets if you don't fancy the idea of a second-hand scraper.

Getting scrubbed

Strigils (Roman cleaning devices) can be tricky to use on your own. Hold the bumpy end and scrape the curved part over your skin.

But if you can afford it, hire an attendant to scrape the muck off your hard-to-reach spots. It's much more relaxing.

Not everyone wants to see a guidebook with naked figures, so I've covered the bathers in our pictures with towels. At the baths, however, nudity is not just accepted but expected.

Top tips for tourists

No. 9: Lost property

There aren't any lockers in the baths – just open shelves – so don't bring anything valuable with you. Thefts are common.

Fortunately you can pay a slave to keep an eye on your belongings, and it's well worth it. You could be in for a rather chilly walk home if a thief decides to pinch your clothes.

A trip to the baths

Rome's a mucky city, so you'll probably be feeling grubby after trudging round the streets for a few hours. But if you're not feeling quite dirty or smelly enough, you can visit the on-site gym first for some weight-lifting or wrestling. That should leave you nice and sweaty.

Wrestling is a great way to work up a sweat. Be careful who you fight, though – not all Romans play fair.

Now, are you ready to sink into a nice, hot bath? Not so fast... Most bath houses have lots of bathrooms, with pools of different temperatures, plus some rooms with no pools at all.

Confusing? Don't worry, I've written out a little guide to the different rooms. Try to visit them in this order, though you could skip a few rooms if you're in a rush.

The *sudatorium*: also known as the *laconicum*, which is basically a sauna. Hot air runs under the floor and inside the walls, so you'll get very hot and work up a good sweat. Try to avoid passing out.

The *caldarium*: the next bath is almost as hot as the *sudatorium*, but with a pool. This is where you use your *strigil*. Or your slave does, if you've hired one.

The *tepidarium*: a large hall with a gently-warmed (or tepid) pool. Here, you can cool off. Ahh, that's a relief.

The *frigidarium*: the final 'bath' is a cool, open-air swimming pool.

Key

Here you can see the layout of a typical bath.

1. The changing rooms
2. The *sudatorium*
3. The *caldarium*
4. Massage room
5. The *tepidarium*
6. The *frigidarium*

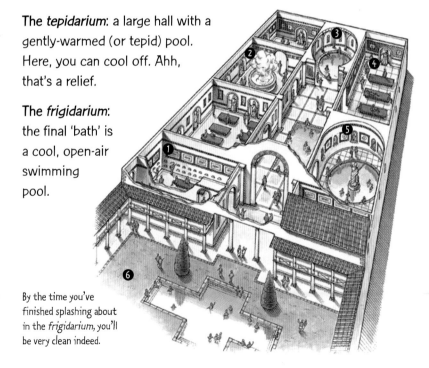

By the time you've finished splashing about in the *frigidarium*, you'll be very clean indeed.

31

Water palaces

For a truly luxurious bathing experience, you should visit Trajan's Baths. Trajan, who was the emperor before Hadrian, built this palatial bathhouse as one of his pet projects. Being about as modest as most emperors, he then named it after himself.

Trajan's Baths are big enough for thousands of bathers, so the noise can be deafening. If you think about how loud it can get in your local pool, imagine the din you'd get from 2,000 people calling, "Look at my dive!" or "Pass the *strigil!*" all at once.

You'll see statues of gods and famous Romans in the niches in the walls.

The hot rooms face southwest, to get the best heat from the afternoon sun.

Romans often do business here. Good idea, getting someone to agree to a deal when they're faint from the heat.

When I first visited, it felt as if I was getting washed in a cathedral, with its marble walls, pillars, and lofty ceilings. On hot days, sunlight streams through windows in the roof so you can sunbathe indoors.

The walls have loads of statues of famous Romans, nestling in niches. These include gods, who seem to me much like modern celebs - they're beautiful, everyone sucks up to them, and they have monster-sized egos. (There's more on Roman gods later.)

Piping hot water

If you think the steam rooms are hot, spare a thought for the slaves working in the tunnels under the baths. It gets unbearably hot down there, and the slaves often faint as they stoke the fires to heat the rooms.

These fires are part of the "*hypocaust*" - the first ever underfloor central heating. The Romans are truly ahead of their time when it comes to creature comforts. Though, it's not so comfy for the slaves, obviously.

Statues at the baths

One of the most impressive statues is known as the Laocöon Group. No, it's not a Roman boy band – it's a sculpture of some people from a story (including a man named Laocöon) being attacked by snakes.

To be honest, I can't recall why they were being attacked. It was probably something to do with an angry god punishing them. Roman gods spend a lot of time in a foul mood.

This diagram shows how the *hypocaust* works.

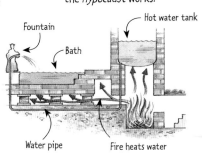

Fountain

Bath

Hot water tank

Water pipe

Fire heats water

Hot air circulates through tunnels under the baths.

Calling all sporty types

Most baths have playing fields attached, and anyone can join in with games. I was never very good at sports at school (history was more my thing) but, in Rome, even I found something I enjoyed. After years of getting into trouble for hand-balls in soccer, I excelled at a Roman type of tennis where you use your hand for a racquet.

Another game I'd never seen before was *harpastum*, an aggressive ball game. The aim is to get the ball from other players. Shoving isn't against the rules: it's a good tactic.

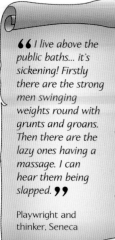

Board games are popular, but often boards aren't used. Players scratch squares into the ground.

There's no such thing as a foul in *harpastum*.

Games counters and dice are available everywhere, if sport's not your thing.

Or you could try a game with less contact, called *trigon*. This involves lots of throwing and catching. Oh, but your head might make contact with the ball if you're slow.

Busy doing nothing

Aaaa...nd relax. After all that running
around, there are plenty of laid-back
activities you can try out at the baths.

   If you're a bookworm, you can read a
scroll in the on-site library. Or you can
take a leisurely stroll through the beautiful,
landscaped gardens. Peckish? You can pick
up a snack at one of the shops. Tense?
Enjoy a massage! Hairy? There's always a
barber around to shear your shaggy locks.

Some Roman make-up contains
poisonous lead. Wear too much
in Rome and you might end up
a very beautiful corpse.

Roman beauty

Female tourists could even get a makeover
by an expert beautician. Just don't ask
what the lotions and potions are
made from. One popular face
mask is a mix of sweat,
oil and dirt, freshly
scraped off the bodies
of burly athletes. That's
not even the worst.
Some beauty products
are actually poisonous,
while others contain
ingredients that I'll leave
up to the imagination.

A Roman beauty kit

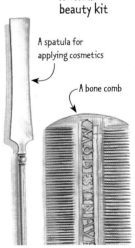

A spatula for
applying cosmetics

A bone comb

A flask of cream for
applying after a bath

Top tips for tourists

No. 11: Early birds

To avoid the worst of the crowds, get up and head out first thing. Too sleepy? It'll be worth it, I promise. An early morning stroll can be very pleasant, and you'll see the sights with some room to move. By mid-morning the streets are packed. That's the time to go for a bath.

Out and about

Although there are no cars in Rome, they do have some shiny-looking chariots. But if you fancy the idea of driving one around Rome, I'm sorry: wheeled vehicles are banned from the city during the day to prevent traffic jams.

A Roman joyrider is stopped in his tracks for driving during the day.

So, you'll be doing most of your visiting on foot, unless you're a night owl. Not that I'd recommend roaming the city's streets at night - not without bodyguards, anyway.

Even during the day, it's no picnic. The back streets are quiet, but you'll be ankle deep in mud. In those alleyways, you'll find yourself mingling with some interesting smells - and some very shady people.

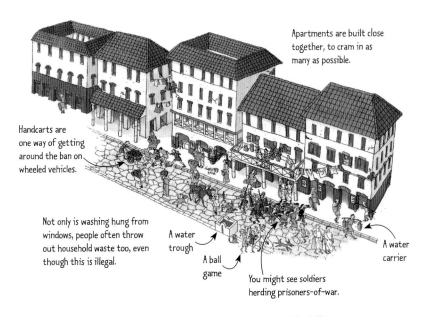

Apartments are built close together, to cram in as many as possible.

Handcarts are one way of getting around the ban on wheeled vehicles.

Not only is washing hung from windows, people often throw out household waste too, even though this is illegal.

A water trough

A ball game

You might see soldiers herding prisoners-of-war.

A water carrier

If you can bear the crowds on the main streets, that's the safest route to take. The roads there are paved - and cleaned on a regular basis. You'll certainly get a feel for the city, and you'll be mingling with plenty of locals too - though possibly too many for comfort.

Be careful crossing roads: night-time traffic wears deep grooves in them, which often fill up with rainwater. You could end up with a very muddy *toga*.

I did find that once I'd tripped over a few dogs and children, I started to enjoy the challenge of staying upright. It's like a city-wide obstacle course.

Hiring a "cab"

If you need a rest, you could hire a litter – a cross between a carriage and a bed, carried by slaves.

Choose carefully, as they range from luxurious ones with cushions, to ones that are falling apart and filthy.

37

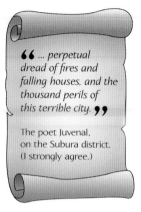

❝ ... perpetual dread of fires and falling houses, and the thousand perils of this terrible city. **❞**

The poet Juvenal, on the Subura district. (I strongly agree.)

The danger zone

Even if you're the tough, streetwise type, I'd avoid the Subura area - at least if you value life, limb and personal hygiene. In a dirty, smelly city, it's the dirtiest, smelliest place of all. It's home to Rome's roughest inhabitants, who think a good day's work means mugging as many people as they can.

Top tips for tourists

No. 12: Pocket watch

Even the nicer parts of Rome are full of thieves. If you don't have a money belt, buy a draw-string purse and hide it in the folds of your *toga* to stop so-called "cutpurses" from slicing the strings. Or invest in this gadget: a metal purse that can only be opened once taken off.

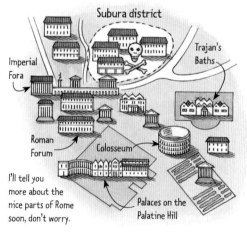

Subura district

Trajan's Baths

Imperial Fora

Roman Forum

Colosseum

I'll tell you more about the nice parts of Rome soon, don't worry.

Palaces on the Palatine Hill

Just don't go there

You'll meet all kinds of criminals in the Subura - if you're foolish enough to ignore my warnings - from gangsters to con-men and thieves. They prey on the unwary - that means you, if you're silly enough to be there.

What if you get lost?

If you get lost in the city, don't panic. Just look for a familiar sight to help you get your bearings. Though if you end up in the Subura district... DO PANIC!

Then, run, very, very fast and far away.

Night watch

You might be comforted to know that the city does have a police force – the Vigiles or Watchmen.

The Vigiles patrol the streets at night, keeping a look out for burglars and other dangerous characters. They also double up as firemen when necessary, which is often.

The nightly traffic jam

When darkness falls, the already crowded city becomes a nightmare of pushing and shoving and shouts of, "Get out of the way you idiot!" as wheeled vehicles are let in.

With no street lighting, you run the risk of being squashed by a cart if you're not careful. Your safest bet is to hire a torch bearer to guide you home.

It's a dirty job

If the streets where you're staying are unbearably filthy, you can complain to the catchily named Quatuorviri Viarum Curandarum - The Four Men Who Look After The Streets. They're the officials responsible for roads, including street cleaning, garbage disposal and traffic. Probably not top of anyone's dream job list.

In some streets the garbage is so deep that local residents have laid stepping stones to get across it.

If you have a headache, a doctor might suggest trepanning, where a hole is drilled in your skull. Only 65% of patients survive. I think I prefer the headache, thanks.

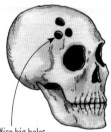

Nice big holes like these take only an hour of continuous drilling.

Getting sick

Time travel to Ancient Rome can be a health hazard, since there are some nasty germs about that your body won't be used to. So it's highly likely you'll feel unwell at some point. What then?

There aren't any public hospitals, but there are plenty of doctors. Unfortunately, few of these have any real training and many do anything they can to get work - even follow potential patients in the street, offering to heal them. (And relieve them of any large sums of money that may be burdening them, of course.)

Natural remedies

Radishes are sometimes used as medicine by doctors. You could always cut out the middle man and eat a large salad instead.

There are some who give sensible advice though. For example, they know that fresh food and exercise are vital for health. Mind you, that's not much use once you're already ill. With a dodgy tummy, the last thing you feel like is a brisk jog.

Roman medicines can be hit and miss, but as they're often made from plants and herbs, they shouldn't do you any harm. Still, you might want to check if they've used another popular ingredient - animal dung.

Medicine and religion

If you visit a doctor in Rome, he might ask you some odd questions as well as asking where it hurts. For example, he might inquire whether you've offended anyone lately. Huh? That was my response when I visited the doctor. But there's a simple - if strange - explanation.

Although medicine here is based partly on trial and error and using remedies that have been proven to work, it's also tied up with religion. It's usual to believe in lots of gods who answer prayers or send curses. Where the cause of a disease isn't known, your doctor is likely to blame your illness on a curse. Mine said I'd been cursed by a baker for insulting his bread.

The doctor god

Asclepius is the god of medicine. He's been known to bring people back from the dead, so curing the sniffles would be easy. Though, some say he died – unusual for a god, and you'd think a doctor god could heal himself.

A votive eye

Rest cure

Some sick people sleep in the medicine god's temple, hoping to dream of a cure. If your dreams are like mine, that means your "cure" might involve being late for an exam or being chased. Other people leave a model of the bit of their body that's hurting (a votive) to show what needs healing, or to say thanks to the god when they're better.

> ❝ I was sick so the doctor hurried over — with ninety students. Ninety cold hands prodded me. I wasn't well before; now I'm really sick. ❞
>
> A famous writer named Martial

41

Surgery

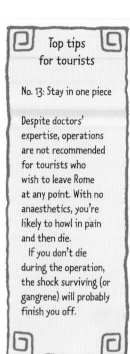

Top tips
for tourists

No. 13: Stay in one piece

Despite doctors'
expertise, operations
are not recommended
for tourists who
wish to leave Rome
at any point. With no
anaesthetics, you're
likely to howl in pain
and then die.

If you don't die
during the operation,
the shock surviving (or
gangrene) will probably
finish you off.

Although a lot of the doctors are highly
suspect, there are some surprisingly skilled
surgeons - especially the army-trained
ones, who'll have plenty of experience of
nasty wounds. The operations they perform
can be quite complex, from setting broken
bones to amputating limbs.

Here's hoping you won't need either
though. If the idea of having someone
chopping up your insides with a scalpel
freaks you out, just imagine being sliced
up while you're wide awake, without any
painkillers. Not even an aspirin.

Apprentice medics get to try out their skills
on real life patients. Let's hope it's not you.

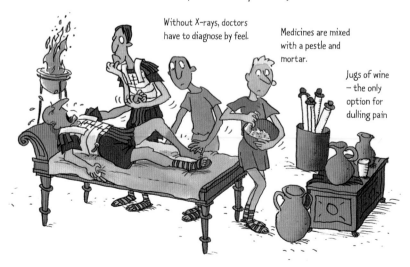

Without X-rays, doctors
have to diagnose by feel.

Medicines are mixed
with a pestle and
mortar.

Jugs of wine
– the only
option for
dulling pain

Part two:
Sightseeing

Sightseeing in Rome doesn't take much effort. Wherever you turn, there's a marble arch or a statue celebrating some bloody battle or other. Bashing foreigners over the head and stealing their land is the quickest path to fame in Rome, it seems.

When it comes to entertainment, be warned. Some Roman shows can get a *little* lively. And by "lively" I mean - well, wait and see.

"Wow!"

"Spectacular!"

"What, ANOTHER statue of Hadrian?"

Provincial visitors

Cynical Roman

At the forum

At the heart of any Roman city lies the forum. This is basically a big market square filled with noisy stalls, with offices, shops, temples, law courts and other impressive-looking buildings all around it.

It's where politicians go to make speeches, lawyers go to do law things, and religious people go to pray - or curse their enemies. It's a great place for gossip, as you'll be surrounded by chattering Romans. Find out who's getting married, who's got a new slave and who's poisoned who.

This forum's full

The main sewer – the Cloaca Maxima – runs under the Roman Forum. It's so large in places, you could sail a boat down it. Emphasis on the *could*.

The city of Rome is so busy that one forum wasn't enough. The original Roman Forum couldn't accomodate all the stalls and crowds - not to mention the hordes of Romans and pesky foreigners on business trips. Mind you, you'll probably be the only tourist there.

To make space - and show off - various emperors built their own *fora* (plural of forum) known as the Imperial Fora. (Read about these on pages 48-49.)

44

The Roman Forum

It's in the Roman Forum that you'll begin to appreciate the majesty of Rome. If you don't, then hundreds of architects and slaves will have wasted a lot of blood, sweat and tears trying to impress you.

The whole place is dripping with history. Take the Rostra - or speaker's platform - where legendary politicians such as Julius Caesar and Cicero gave speeches. It's also where Cicero's head and hands were displayed after he was murdered. (Roman political debates could get heated.)

KEY

1. Basilica Julia
2. Basilica Aemilia
3. Regia
4. Temple of Saturn
5. Shrine of Venus Cloacina
6. Rostra
7. Curia
8. Temple of Castor
9. Temple of Concord
10. Temple of Vespasian
11. Temple of Caesar
12. Tabularium
13. Lapis Niger
14. House of the Vestal Virgins

The Roman Forum

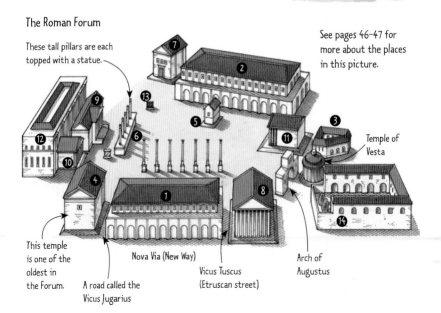

These tall pillars are each topped with a statue.

See pages 46–47 for more about the places in this picture.

Temple of Vesta

This temple is one of the oldest in the Forum.

A road called the Vicus Jugarius

Nova Via (New Way)

Vicus Tuscus (Etruscan street)

Arch of Augustus

Trials can get very noisy, since lawyers hire crowds to cheer them on – and boo their opponents.

Here's some more about the sights in the Roman Forum...

Basilica Julia and Basilica Aemillia: court houses where you can watch trials in action. Trials can turn into real soap operas, revealing juicy scandals.

Regia: the headquarters of the chief priest of Rome. If you wanted to cause a real stir, you could appear at the window, dressed as a god and carrying a flashlight. He might think you're a god and fall at your feet. Alternatively, he might kill you for being a blasphemous sorceror, so.... maybe not.

The festival of Saturnalia is held in December. Masters and slaves swap places for the day and life becomes a little topsy-turvy.

Temple of Saturn: Saturn was said to have taught the Romans how to farm. The festival of Saturnalia's named after him, too.

Shrine of Venus Cloacina: dedicated to Venus Cloacina, goddess of the sewer. Romans have gods for the strangest things.

Rostra: the platform used by politicians to make speeches to their adoring public.

Senators are usually over 30, though boys as young as 18 can get in if they do something amazing for the city. Usually this means conquering foreigners.

Curia (Senate House): The senators used to govern here, but the emperor's in charge now. If he says, "Jump!", the Senate says, "How high?" (Although some of the older senators might say, "Eh, speak up?")

46

Temple of Castor: dedicated to Castor and Pollux, gods who supposedly help the Romans in battle. Given how mighty the Roman army is, they seem to do their job.

Temple of Concord: But it's not all war, war, war. This temple is for a peace goddess.

Vespasian's temple: built in memory of Emperor Vespasian. Romans like to think of dead emperors as gods. Live emperors often have a similar opinion of themselves.

Temple of Caesar: dedicated to the military dictator Julius Caesar. Inside there's a statue of him with a star on his head. But not everyone thought he was a superstar: he was murdered by his enemies, not far from where the temple stands today.

Tabularium: the public record office, where state records are kept. And - often - lost.

Lapis Niger: a slab of black marble, said to mark the grave of Romulus. It's covered in curses, threatening anyone who touches it with torment. I dare you to give it a poke.

House of the Vestal Virgins: six holy women known as Vestal Virgins have to keep a fire constantly burning here. It's thought that if it ever goes out, disaster will befall Rome. So, no pressure then, girls.

Alas, I think I am becoming a god.

Emperor Vespasian cracks a joke while dying – that's what the writer Suetonius claims he said, anyway.

Many people believe Caesar's soul went up to heaven in the form of a comet in the sky.

You're grounded!

Vestal Virgins can't get married, and if one is caught with a boyfriend, she is literally grounded – buried alive. But if they stay single, they have more freedom than most Roman women: they can even vote in elections.

The Imperial Fora

Dictators and emperors like to show off by putting their faces on coins. This one shows Julius Caesar's face.

In Rome, you've got loads of *fora* to choose from if you want to combine a little culture with a lot of shopping.

The great military dictator Caesar built a new forum in 51BC. Over the years, the emperors Augustus, Vespasian, Nerva and Trajan followed suit. Their plan? Romans could shop 'til they dropped, while contemplating their rulers' generosity.

Plan of the Imperial Fora

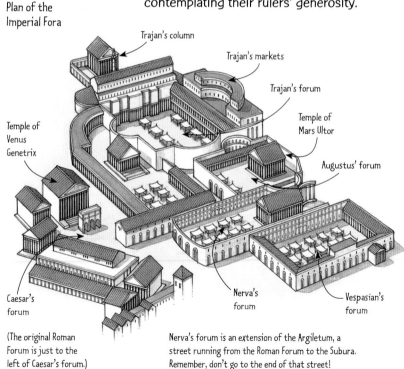

Trajan's column

Trajan's markets

Trajan's forum

Temple of Mars Ultor

Temple of Venus Genetrix

Augustus' forum

Caesar's forum

Nerva's forum

Vespasian's forum

(The original Roman Forum is just to the left of Caesar's forum.)

Nerva's forum is an extension of the Argiletum, a street running from the Roman Forum to the Subura. Remember, don't go to the end of that street!

48

Caesar's forum

To make room for his forum, Caesar had to buy and demolish an entire street of houses. It's an impressive sight, but it cost a bomb, and I wonder if it was worth it for Caesar? Even though many citizens loved it, it didn't stop him from being murdered by jealous senators who thought he was getting too big for his boots.

You can reach Caesar's forum via the original Forum. Dominating the scene is the Temple of the goddess Venus Genetrix. Caesar claimed he was descended from her, so I'm not entirely surprised people thought he had too high an opinion of himself.

In front of the temple is a statue of Caesar on his horse, displaying some unusual hooves - they're cloven. It was said that split hooves were a sign from the gods that Caesar would rule the world, but it just makes me think of devils.

Close by is an underground prison where, legend has it, Saint Peter and Saint Paul (from the Bible) were prisoners. Many Christians had a terrible time in Rome. Some were even fed to vicious, starving lions.

Cleopatra the goddess

Inside the Temple of Venus Genetrix there's a statue of Venus, based on the Egyptian queen, Cleopatra. Caesar fell madly in love with Cleopatra, so it's no wonder he thought she looked like a goddess.

Venus is the goddess of love, beauty and motherhood.

Saint Peter is said to have made water flow from the earth to baptize guards and inmates.

49

A tour of the fora

After Caesar's forum, you could check out the *fora* of Vespasian, Trajan and Augustus. They're all very impressive and beautiful, but take my advice: don't take photos, unless you're sneaky. You'll get some very funny looks. And soldiers might even think you're a sorceror wielding a magical box that makes pictures out of thin air and kidnap you as a novelty gift for the emperor. (Yes, I am giving you this warning from experience. I had to bribe the guards a LOT of money to let me out.)

Tasteful gifts, total tack

Trajan looks at plans for his forum. It's the biggest and most spectacular of the *fora*.

Speaking of money, you'll find plenty of bargains in the *fora*. For a classy gift, you could pick up some art, such as a vase painted with scenes from Greek myths. They're often violent, though, so don't give one to a relative with a nervous disposition.

You could also buy yourself a brightly painted model of Emperor Hadrian to show just how much you admire him. And you'd really have to be a fan - because they're hideous. Then again, it wouldn't be a real souvenir if it wasn't a little tacky.

Trajan the winner

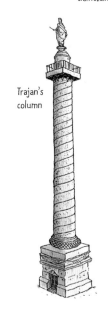

Trajan's column

In the emperor Trajan's forum, you'll see Trajan's Column – you could hardly miss it. It stands 38m (125ft) tall and offers a whacking great marble-clad reminder of what an amazing soldier Trajan was. It's covered in pictures of just some of many the battles that he won.

Trajan's forum is proof of how mighty he was in battle: he paid for it using the loot he "confiscated" after vanquishing various foes. It's the biggest and swankiest of the *fora*, with some magnificent boutiques. Just his way of saying, "Buy shiny things and look at pretty statues and think how great your emperor is, you insignificant worms!"

War and peace

In Vespasian's forum, you can see the splendid-looking Temple of Peace. Mind you, they've got a nerve calling it a "peace" temple, given that it commemorates giving the Jews a good kicking in Judea.

I'm sure many of the people conquered by the Romans thought their attitude to peace was a bit rich. One British chieftain apparently remarked, bitterly: "They make a desolation and they call it peace."

Top tips
for tourists

No. 14: The War-um

Military buffs should head for the forum of Augustus. There, you can have a look at all kinds of weapons in the Temple of Mars Ulto. Mars is the Roman god of war – if you're lucky, you might see a military parade.

The games of death

Roll up! Roll up! It's the goriest show on Earth! Yes, ladies and gentlemen, if you want to experience everything that Rome has to offer, even the unpleasant parts, then head down to the Flavian Amphitheatre (or Colosseum) for "the Games" - featuring the most violent spectator sports in history.

Gasp, as fierce gladiators fight to the death! Shudder, as a mighty lion pits its strength against an elephant! Faint, as the blood splatters across the arena...

Freebies for all

If I haven't already put you off, there's one good thing about the Games - the tickets are paid for by your generous emperor, Hadrian. So you can always leave if it gets too much. Enter the stadium through the arch number on your ticket.

The Games are held at the Colosseum

Roman Forum

Trajan's Baths

Colosseum

Gladiator Training School

Temple of Claudius

Palaces on the Palatine Hill

Circus Maximus

There's more about the Circus Maximus on pages 53-54. If you're afraid of clowns, don't worry. It's not that sort of circus.

A lovely place to die

The Colosseum is a stunning stadium which can house up to 50,000 blood-crazed spectators. (You should probably sit somewhere in the *cavea* - see key on right.)

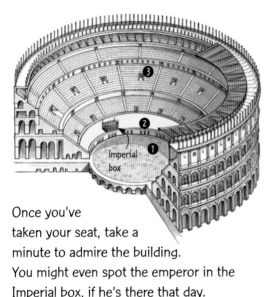

Once you've taken your seat, take a minute to admire the building. You might even spot the emperor in the Imperial box, if he's there that day.

If it's hot, slaves hoist a vast sunshade called a *velarium* across some of the seats. It doesn't cover the arena though, as bright sunlight is needed to see what's going on. So the gladiators have to sweat it out as they fight to the death.

Before you know it, there'll be a blare of trumpets, and the Games will begin.

Key

❶ The arena: the name comes from the *harena* (sand) on the floor. Beneath is a network of tunnels, storing scenery, wild animals, victims and machinery to hoist them all into the arena.

❷ The *podium*: a broad terrace on the arena wall. The best spot is for the emperor; the other seats are for senators and foreign ambassadors.

❸ The *cavea*: this is divided into three tiers of seats. Men sit closest to the front, then women. Slaves have to stand at the back.

❝ *He entertained the people with 320 single combats.* ❞

The author Plutarch on the gladiatorial combats that helped make Julius Caesar popular. Just imagine a world leader trying that now.

Learning how to write is a handy skill for an elephant at the games. Otherwise, this elephant might have to fight angry rhinos.

The warm-up act

The Games usually begin with some light-hearted acts, such as acrobats, as well as a procession with music and dancing.

The animal acts that follow are far stranger: panthers pulling chariots, people wrestling alligators and elephants tracing Latin phrases in the sand with their trunks – at least, someone told me that happens, I haven't seen that act myself. If this already sounds too much like animal cruelty, I really wouldn't stay for the rest...

The show begins

The real show often kicks off with vicious battles between wild animals. Ever wondered who'd win in a fight between an elephant and a rhino? Or a tiger and a lion? This could be your chance to find out.

Then, you might see some criminals being eaten by lions. These lions are starved until they're so hungry they could eat a horse. (But a man would do nicely, thanks.)

One gimmick is to release savage animals through a trapdoor in the floor, to eat whoever's in the arena. The Roman crowd loves it – but I had nightmares for weeks.

Gladiators

The stars of the show are the mighty gladiators. Many of these professional fighters are slaves, while others are poor free men who see it as a path to a better life - if they survive long enough. Some only last a few fights, but others do win fame, fortune and (for slaves) freedom.

This gladiator is starting to regret his career choice.

Ladies love these hunky heroes, and men want to be them. (Some ladies want to be them, too, but female gladiators are rare.)

Thracian: carries a curved dagger and a small, round shield.

Five types of gladiator

Samnite: is heavily armed with a great big sword and a shield.

Murmillo: also heavily armed; wears a helmet crowned with a fish.

Secutor – "pursuer": fights with sword; wears helmet, shield and protection on his sword arm.

Retiarius – "net fighter": fights with a net and trident; has one arm protected.

Thumbs up

If a gladiator fights well but loses, he can appeal to the emperor to spare his life. He has to hope the emperor is impressed and gives him the thumbs up – this means he lives.

But if the emperor doesn't like his style, or if he's in a bad mood, then it's thumbs down... DEATH!

Chariot racing

Romans love a day at the races. The chariot races, that is, where chariots rush around a track, pulled along by teams of horses. It's not as violent as the Games, but it wouldn't be a Roman sport without a little danger. Or, let's be honest, a LOT.

As the chariots thunder round the track, accidents are inevitable. So are "accidents" - as in, "Oops, silly me, I rammed your chariot so hard its wheels fell off."

Don't expect clowns

Chariot races happen at an arena called a *circus* - nothing to do with clowns and custard pies; it's just the Latin for a chariot racing track. The most famous is the Circus Maximus, which seats 250,000.

Anyone can go for free - Romans have come to expect a lot of freebies, and there'd be trouble if the free fun stopped. The emperor and other politicians have to keep the people happy at all costs.

The Circus Maximus stands in front of the palaces on the Palatine Hill not far from the river.

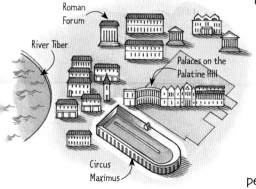

Roman Forum

River Tiber

Palaces on the Palatine Hill

Circus Maximus

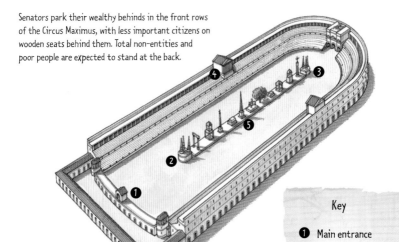

Senators park their wealthy behinds in the front rows of the Circus Maximus, with less important citizens on wooden seats behind them. Total non-entities and poor people are expected to stand at the back.

Key

1. Main entrance
2. Central barrier
3. Turning posts
4. Imperial box
5. *Obelisk* (a decorative pillar)

As you pass through the gleaming marble entrance, you'll be mobbed by a host of snack merchants trying to sell you pastries and other titbits.

Even if you're not hungry, it's a good idea to stock up before you go in - or you'll spend the day fighting your way through crowds, rather than watching the races.

When you've got your provisions, try to grab a seat near either end of the course. You'll get the best view here. The places where the chariots have to turn are usually the most exciting parts of the race, and the greatest test of a charioteer's skill.

As the riders turn, crashes – known as 'shipwrecks' – are common. The crowd loves them.

57

Whipping up a frenzy

Before the race, there's a musical parade, and at the rear you'll see the VIP who's in charge of the races that day. This is often a consul, but if it's the emperor, the crowd will go crazy. If you think people get excited about Barack Obama, you should hear the explosion of applause Hadrian gets.

This picture of circus musicians is made of tiny pieces of stone. The technique is known as *mosaic*.

The emperor (or the official in charge that day) drops a white cloth – the signal to start.

Before the races begin, why not pick a team to cheer for? You could think up some juicy insults for the other teams, too.

But I'd check who you're sitting by before you start cheering or jeering. Rivalry is fierce and you don't want to be shouting, "Come on you Reds! The Whites' horses are donkeys!" if you're sitting by a gang of burly Whites fans. If they're sensitive souls, they might overreact - with their fists.

"...and they're off!"

As Emperor Hadrian drops a white cloth, the chariot drivers lash their horses into action. The chariots tear off round the track and the crowd goes wild.

As the drivers swerve around the bend, you might see the first casualties. Members of one team often gang up on drivers from the other teams, to try to force them off the track. (Fair play? That's for losers and weaklings.) If a driver falls, he has to crawl away quickly, or be trampled.

Sweet, sweet victory

Seven nail-biting laps and much cheering later, the winner is presented with a palm leaf, gold and instant fame. Even the horses can become celebrities, though I doubt they appreciate it. (There are only so many oats a horse can eat, after all.)

1... 2...3 dolphins

Laps are counted with markers in the shape of golden eggs or golden dolphins.
I couldn't discover why these particular symbols were chosen. Mysterious...

The palm leaf of victory – it doesn't look like much, but it's a chariot driver's dream come true.

Drivers wrap the reins around their waist, so they have to carry a knife to cut themselves free if they take a tumble.

Non-violent fun

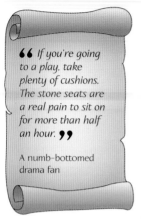

❝ If you're going to a play, take plenty of cushions. The stone seats are a real pain to sit on for more than half an hour. ❞

A numb-bottomed drama fan

I don't want to give you the wrong idea, though. The Romans *can* have a good time without seeing someone trampled to death. Plays are very popular, for example.

The Theatrum Pompeii is a spectacular place to take in a show – for free. You might even be offered money to applaud extra-loud. Roman patrons of the arts (*a.k.a.* ambitious politicians) will try every trick in the book to ensure *their* play succeeds.

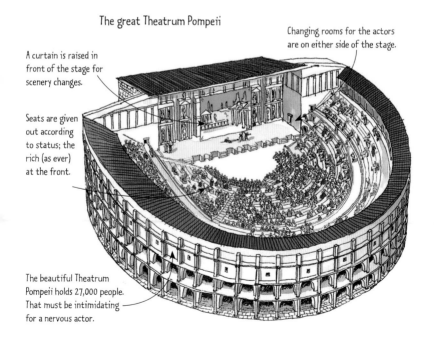

The great Theatrum Pompeii

Changing rooms for the actors are on either side of the stage.

A curtain is raised in front of the stage for scenery changes.

Seats are given out according to status; the rich (as ever) at the front.

The beautiful Theatrum Pompeii holds 27,000 people. That must be intimidating for a nervous actor.

High drama?

Do you think that going to see a play means high culture and good taste? Not in Rome. More likely, it'll involve lots of falling over, rude jokes and actors behaving like monkeys who've eaten too much sugar and then raided the fancy dress box.

Silence is not golden for Roman audiences. Feel free to laugh, cry, shout, and duck when critics throw things at the actors.

This is partly because of the size of most playhouses in the city. With an audience of thousands, there'd be no point doing anything subtle, tasteful and sophisticated. The people at the back would fall asleep.

Getting involved

At home, you may be used to watching plays in respectful silence. Not so here. The audience screams, boos, hisses and more. Instead of writing reviews, critics keep up a running commentary during the show. Sometimes, riots can break out as people debate the merits of the actors.

One key tip if you're shy: avoid sitting close to the front. While very important Romans will be safe, *you* might be dragged up to play an unexpected, undignified role.

Top tips for tourists

No. 18: 'Tis the season

Drama-buffs note: plays are only put on from April to November, and only on certain days. If you're there out of season, try some street drama. This can be total chaos, with members of the public joining in – both willingly and unwillingly.

Key to costumes

Actors' robes are designed to show who they are playing:

Red robes mean the person is poor.

Purple robes indicate a rich citizen.

The costumes of elderly characters tend to be white.

Slave characters wear simple tunics.

Actors playing young characters will wear brighter clothes.

Dumbing down

In the early days, many Roman plays were tragedies – that is, dramas full of gloomy life-lessons, such as: "Everything that can go wrong will go wrong. And then everyone will die horribly."

They were also very long, with twisty plots. Add a noisy audience, and you ended up with a miserable, confusing night out.

Thankfully, plays in Hadrian's time are a lot simpler and cheerier. Even if you don't speak Latin, you'll be able to follow them.

Oooh, naughty!

Comedies are the most popular shows, especially ones with lots of rude jokes. They tend to involve people falling in love and falling over a lot. If you want something more cultured, classical Greek tragedies are still performed – but that's three (confused) hours of your life you'll never get back.

Plays usually have a live musical soundtrack. Lyres, like this one, are popular. It's basically a mini harp.

That's just typical

In the 21st century, if you say that a character in a play or a movie is a stereotype, it's a criticism. But in Ancient Rome, it's a good thing. To make things clear and easy to understand on stage, the characters are simple stereotypes, such as "wise old man" or "smiling fool".

The actors' faces can't be seen from high up, so they wear masks with exaggerated expressions. The masks also show whether the character is male or female, since the actors are always male.

Acting is NOT a profession for respectable citizens and many actors are slaves. Still, star actors have lots of fans. With this in mind, women can't sit near the stage in case they (gasp) fall in love and run off with a slave.

Even naughtier

For something completely, shockingly different, try a mime show. The actors don't wear masks - and even women are allowed to take part. In fact, in mime, pretty much anything goes, and they're usually very, very rude.

If Brad Pitt or Johnny Depp were around in Roman times, they'd have to wear these.

Top tips for tourists

No. 19: Dead good

Don't think going to a play is a soft option. Actors have to compete with the gory Games, remember.

So, to add spice, some plays have real live bloodshed. It's not completely unknown for criminals to be killed onstage – in the interests of dramatic realism, of course.

Under construction

BANG! THWACK! BANG! Sorry, what? You
can't hear over the noise of the hammering
and MIND YOUR HEAD! yelling of the
builders in Rome. It sometimes seems more
like a construction site than a city. If you
spend a while here, you'll see new buildings
shooting up all around you.

Many Roman buildings are breathtaking
feats of engineering - from huge aqueducts
that supply Rome with water, to the vast
arenas that satisfy the people's hunger for
brutal entertainment.

Here are some Greeks
building pillars. Watch out
for Roman copycats, guys!

Greek is good

Roman architects know that they're not
just creating arenas or aqueducts - they're
sending a message: "Rome is great! Rome
is rich! Rome will invade you if you
don't behave!" But though "Hurrah for
Rome!" is the message behind Roman
buildings, the style is very much
Greek. The Romans see the Greeks
as incredibly cultured. In fact, they
were so impressed, they
invaded them and stole
their ideas.

Ungreek ideas

Roman architects also make tunnel vaults - arches placed side by side to form a tunnel. For a little variation, these were pinched from the Egyptians. But the Romans make much better, safer ones.

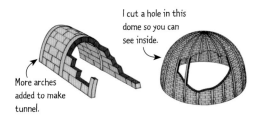

I cut a hole in this dome so you can see inside.

More arches added to make tunnel.

One all-Roman design feature is the dome, which you'll see in stunning temples and flashy palaces, often magnificently painted.

A guide to columns

Columns are everywhere in Rome. If you're in a spotting mood, keep this page open and see how many you can see of each style. Most use Greek or Greek-like styles.

Only the "Tuscan" style of pillar is home-grown, but it's the least impressive of the lot. It tends to be used only for army camps and prisons. With luck, you won't be seeing that one much.

Column spotting

How many of these pillar styles can you spot in Rome?

Corinthian

Ionic

Composite

Doric

Tuscan

Temple in progress

A temple known as the Pantheon - Greek
for "temple of all the gods" - was built
years ago in Rome. But one of Rome's
frequent fires wrecked it, so Emperor
Hadrian is currently rebuilding it. Some
people claim he's designing it, too, but I
think that's just hype, personally.

It's going to have the largest dome in
history (well, Ancient Roman history) and
should be stunning once it's finished.

As the Greek name suggests, parts of its
design were inspired by Greek temples. The
new version will still be Greek-looking from
the front, but its insides will be far more
Roman in style.

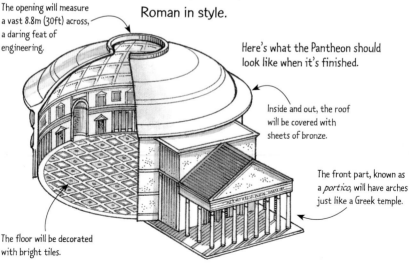

The opening will measure
a vast 8.8m (30ft) across,
a daring feat of
engineering.

Here's what the Pantheon should
look like when it's finished.

Inside and out, the roof
will be covered with
sheets of bronze.

The front part, known as
a *portico*, will have arches
just like a Greek temple.

The floor will be decorated
with bright tiles.

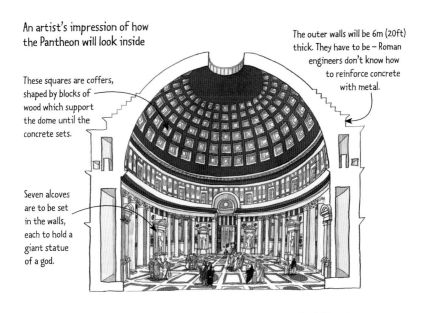

An artist's impression of how the Pantheon will look inside

The outer walls will be 6m (20ft) thick. They have to be – Roman engineers don't know how to reinforce concrete with metal.

These squares are coffers, shaped by blocks of wood which support the dome until the concrete sets.

Seven alcoves are to be set in the walls, each to hold a giant statue of a god.

It'd be a shame not to see this temple when it's finished. Perhaps it would be worth taking a brief trip forward in time, to around the year 150, so you can see it in its full, finished glory?

Then you'll be able to see its beautiful ceiling, showing off the best of Roman engineering. An opening called the *oculus* (eye) in the roof will let sunlight stream through. Stay a few hours to watch the light move around the dome as the day passes. Avoid wet days, though, when rain will pour through instead.

Hadrian 4 Greece

The Greek style is normal in Roman architecture. But for Hadrian, it goes deeper – he's nuts for all things Greek, from people to philosophy.

He's such a fan that he even grew a beard to look more Greek. Some sarcastic senators nicknamed him "the Greekling" because of his obsession.

Morbid tourism

Everybody dies. But in Rome, people tend to do it sooner rather than later. Many children don't make it past their 5th birthday. Even if they survive into adulthood, most people don't live much past fifty - even the rich and well-fed.

So, chances are you'll probably see at least one important funeral procession during your stay. Funerals are a chance for a wealthy family to show off.

The body itself is carried in a solemn procession, on an open litter. Sometimes it's propped up, so people can see which well-known person has died - like a waxwork museum, only with a corpse.

Funeral procession

Trumpeters lead the rest of the procession if the funeral is for an adult.

Actors wearing masks represent the dead person's famous ancestors. Even death won't stop Romans from showing off.

Dozens of musicians and professional mourners join family and friends, accompanying the body on its final journey.

This poor creature doesn't know what's in store – black animals are included in the procession, to be sacrificed at the end.

68

When you die in Rome

Not you, personally - I mean when a Roman dies - the body is washed and covered in oil. If the person was a senator, he's dressed in his official robes. Then the body is covered in flowers and wreaths and put on display for a few days so visitors can pay their final respects.

On the day of the funeral, the procession heads first to the forum for speeches praising the deceased. Then, the body is carried out of the city to be buried or cremated - ever since Julius Caesar's time, it's been illegal to do either inside the city.

Funeral customs

After death, the Romans believe you're ferried by boat to an "underworld" known as *Hades*. (This is yet another idea they pinched from the Greeks.) Because of this, every dead body has a coin placed under its tongue, to pay the ferryman.

Also, their hands are filled with cakes to feed Cerberus: the dog who guards *Hades*. He has three heads and isn't the sort of dog you'd pick as a family pet. Or if he is, I'd rather not meet your family.

Here lies...

Tombstones are carved by skilled craftsmen.

The dead man's image is carved on the stone.

An image of his dead son is added — they're buried together — and their names are carved.

A coin such as this one pays for the last journey a Roman ever makes.

69

To the
Colosseum

The Appian
Way

The Appian Way

Many tombs lie along the Appian Way, or Via Appia, the main road leading out of Rome to the south.

Most of the tombs are elaborately carved and you can learn a great deal about people's lives just from reading their tombstones.

To take a trip along the Via Appia, you can pick up a litter or a carriage from the stables at one of the gates leading out of the city. Not all stables are reliable, so inspect your horse before setting off. They may try to saddle you (sorry) with an ancient animal that can hardly carry its own weight, never mind yours.

Some people say that the ghosts of Romans who didn't have proper burials haunt this road.

As a rule of thumb, the bigger the tombstone, the richer the person.

The Appian Way is 122 miles (196 kms) long and sees a constant stream of traffic.

Rest stops

If you go too far to turn back that day, don't worry. There are places where you can spend the night and give your horse a rest along the route - think of these as the Roman equivalent of motels.

To the port of Ostia

70

Secret meetings

Some of the tombs around Rome are underground resting places known as catacombs. They're made up of shadowy passageways and damp, silent rooms.

If you're tempted to take a look, be careful. These chambers are used for secret meetings by banned groups, such as Christians. If you stumble in on one of these, leave quickly or you risk arrest.

A spooky place to hold a prayer meeting, isn't it?

Cremation vs. burial

Most funerals end with a cremation on a blazing pyre. The ashes are then buried in a decorative urn. (I'm not sure how the underworld's guard dog is meant to eat the cakes provided if they're burned up.)

Top tips
for tourists

No. 23: Crocodile tears

If you fancy making some extra cash during your trip, you could work as a professional mourner. You'll be given a tear bottle to catch your tears. But don't spill any – mourners are paid by the amount they shed. To make sure the tears flow, you might find it helps to go via a market and pick up a raw onion first.

A tear bottle

66 At the funeral of a driver for the Reds, one fan leaped onto the funeral pyre. 99

Pliny the Elder, on seriously obsessed racing fans

Soldiers on parade

If you're lucky, you might be in Rome on the day of a military parade. These are usually held to celebrate a Roman victory.

Under Hadrian, this means they're rare. That's not because he loses wars: he just doesn't start many, as he's not interested in making the Empire bigger. It's already a nightmare to keep it under control as it is.

But even though there aren't many victory marches, there'll be a parade on Hadrian's birthday. (Ask a Roman when that is, as I'm afraid I don't know.)

If you're lucky enough to catch a parade, it's an uplifting sight. Maybe you'll feel moved to join the army yourself.

The general who won the battle rides in a chariot, lapping up the cheers and whistles of his adoring fans.

See the pretty sun glinting off all the shiny weapons. And feel grateful you're not facing them in battle.

72

Romans are winners

At the front of the parade come the senators, trying to look as important as they possibly can, even if they didn't lift a finger in the battle itself. They're the brains behind the operation - or so they think.

Further back, you'll see soldiers and wagons with people acting out battles from the war. Look out for the general - he'll be in a flashy chariot, puffing out his chest as if to say, "Thank you, you're too kind... well, perhaps not too kind. I am rather amazing."

Roman soldiers on the march are a scary sight. Even when it's only a parade, it can make you feel nervous, watching row after row of them march past, with the sun glinting on their sharp and very pointy-looking weapons.

Don't get smug

In a parade, a slave holds a victory wreath over the winning general's head. But to stop him feeling too pleased with himself - or getting ideas about becoming Emperor - the slave also keeps whispering in his ear: "Remember: you're only human."

Lots of lovely loot

War, what is it good for? Stealing gold from foreigners, that's what.

As part of the procession, you'll see the treasures that have been "liberated" from the enemy... then, the poor enemy prisoners, looking miserable. (It's not a proper Roman victory parade if you don't humiliate the losers.)

73

Don't forget we won

All over Rome, you can spot huge arches, known as Triumphal Arches, which were built (you guessed it) in memory of a triumph on the battlefield. Look out for the Emperor Trajan's arch on the Via Appia.

Want to feel small and unimportant? Stand beside a triumphal arch. They are gigantic.

How a real queen dies

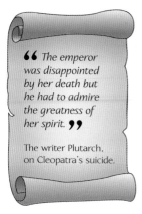

66 *The emperor was disappointed by her death but he had to admire the greatness of her spirit.* **99**

The writer Plutarch, on Cleopatra's suicide.

In the Roman Forum, look for the Arch of Emperor Augustus. It was built to celebrate the emperor's victory over Mark Antony (a consul) and Cleopatra, the Queen of Egypt.

But before the victory parade, Cleopatra and Anthony killed themselves. So Augustus never got to parade the losers around Rome in chains. Poor little emperor – the world's smallest violin is playing a sad song for him.

Part three:

Shopping in Rome

You'll probably want to buy yourself some souvenirs to take home. After all, it would be nice to have some proof of your journey through time.

So, what kinds of things can you buy that are typically Roman, that you can't get anywhere else - or any-when-else? Where should you shop? Where will you find the best bargains? And how do you avoid getting ripped off by unscrupulous merchants? (They're everywhere in Rome.)

"I wouldn't buy anything from that glass-blower!"

I agree with the Roman lady on the left.

Hey, small spender

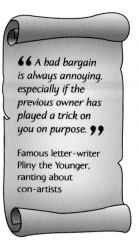

❞ *A bad bargain is always annoying, especially if the previous owner has played a trick on you on purpose.* ❟

Famous letter-writer Pliny the Younger, ranting about con-artists

Whether you want souvenirs or a snack, you can find bargains in the markets and shops of Rome. You'll find the more exclusive boutiques around the edges of the *fora* while everyday goods are found in ground-floor outlets all over the city.

There probably won't be a sign outside these, but each store will have its wares spread out so you can tell what's on sale.

Don't be surprised if most of the other shoppers are slaves. Very few well-to-do Romans do their own shopping, unless they're buying something fun, such as a necklace. What would a *slave* know about posh jewels, after all?

You can buy anything from bacon to pots and pans to magic spells in Roman shops.

Opening hours

In Rome, artificial lighting means spluttery oil lamps, so Romans make the most of the daylight. Stores open early and shut at dusk. Some may close over lunchtime, too, at least in the hottest summer months. Not a bad time to take a siesta yourself, Roman-style.

Made while you wait

A lot of what you can buy will be made
on the premises - from pots and furniture
to loaves of bread. You can even watch
your goods being made. But stand well
back if there's any hammering or melting.
Health and safety regulations haven't been
invented yet.

A mobile knife sharpening stall
– as many Romans carry cutlery
around, these come in handy.

You can even buy
hand-crafted tools.
But I imagine you
won't be doing
much DIY, unless
your roof falls in.

There aren't any factories full of
machines, so everything's made by
hand, from pots to chariots.

Footwear and foot-care

If you wear out your sandals walking
around Rome, just visit a shoemaker. They'll
measure you up and make new ones on
the spot. If your feet are aching, pop into a
pharmacist to buy some soothing ointment
or - if you're feeling particularly rich and
gullible - a magic spell.

Let your feet breathe in the
latest Roman sandal styles.

A shopper's paradise

Fed up of being jostled by slaves and
other riff-raff? Then head to the exclusive
boutiques in the arcades around each
forum. Prices are steep, but you'll find
exquisite objects there. You'll also be
browsing with senators and their wives.
Look down your nose and be rude to the
salespeople, and you'll fit right in.

Personalized perfume

The Vicus Tuscus is probably the best-
known shopping street. Here, you'll find
the finest imported silks. Close by are
specialist perfumiers, who will create a
tailor-made scent for you. If you want to
admire yourself, you can buy polished silver
mirrors - they don't make glass ones yet.

Why smell just
like everyone
else? Mix your
own scent
instead.

Stop thieves

There are pick-pockets everywhere, so one
very useful purchase is a lockable casket for
valuables. It comes with a key designed to
be worn as a ring.

Yes, it's literally a keyring. (There's a
picture of one on the left there.)

Keyrings are made of iron, not
silver or gold. They'd be too
soft – and rather easy for
thieves to bend open.

Glassware

If you want to be in with the in-crowd in Rome, you could buy some glassware. Glass is so expensive that only the richest Romans will own any. If you want to impress your fellow shoppers, perhaps you could talk loudly about just how much glassware you have at home: "My whole room's simply littered with perfume flasks, darling!"

Glassblowers have to have a good pair of lungs. I bet they still get dizzy sometimes.

As you browse, you'll see glass in every possible shade, except for the completely see-through kind - that hasn't been invented yet.

Be an art collector

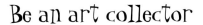

Another current shopping craze is for Greek art. That's not surprising, given that the emperor's a fan of Greek things, and everyone wants to be more like him.

All of Rome is collecting antique Greek vases at the moment, so you're bound to find something in your price range. Watch out, though - some of these "antiques" were made last week. Though, of course, once you're back home, anything you buy in Rome will qualify as an antique anyway.

Mind your back

For a truly impressive souvenir, you could invest in a marble statue or a bronze bust of the emperor. But it might prove difficult to take home.

79

Fancy materials

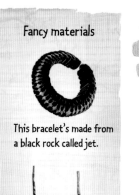

This bracelet's made from a black rock called jet.

These earrings are made from clusters of pearls. Those babies look *heavy*.

Shiny stuff

In the old Roman Forum, there's a street of silversmiths and goldsmiths where you can buy exclusive items made from gold and silver. All the pieces are unique, and you could even get them engraved. If you want the engraving in any language other than Latin, you'll probably have to spell it all... out... very... slowly.

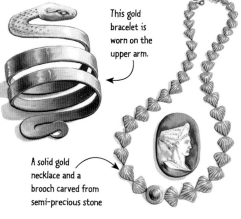

This gold bracelet is worn on the upper arm.

A solid gold necklace and a brooch carved from semi-precious stone

You'll notice well-off Roman women don't believe in the subtle look when it comes to gold and jewels. It's amazing they can even move with all those bracelets, brooches, necklaces and tiaras weighing them down. It's a good thing that wealthy Roman women tend to get carried everywhere.

Strange beauty

You might think only the super-famous have personal make-up artists. But in Rome, most wealthy women have their own slave – called an *ornatrix* – to make them up each day. Roman ladies like their makeup like they like their jewels: visible from a distance and as subtle as a slap round the face.

The cosmetics on sale in Rome use all-natural ingredients such as chalk, wine, soggy bread and bone marrow. That almost sounds like a meal, but not a very nice one.

> 66 *Don't apply lotions made with deer marrow in public, and I don't approve of publicly cleaning your teeth: it makes you pretty, but isn't pretty to watch.* 99
>
> The poet Ovid gives "helpful" advice about how to look good.

Books without covers

Romans use scrolls (rolled sheets of paper written by hand) rather than books. You can buy these from the Argiletum, by the Basilica Aemilia. There are no printing machines to speed things along. Each scroll is copied out by slaves.

People are hired to read aloud to the slaves who copy out scrolls – an ideal job if you're an avid book (or scroll) worm.

No two scrolls are the same. Especially since not all scribes can spell.

81

Top tips
for tourists

No. 27: An early start

If you want the freshest fruit and veg, try to be at the market as it opens – your fellow shoppers, mostly slaves, will be up well before dawn. Or if you want a lie in, hire some slaves to do your shopping for you.

Fruit and veg

For a more down-to-earth shopping experience, leave the exclusive stores of the *fora* behind and head for the market stalls located in the middle of each forum.

As you approach, you'll hear a babble of voices - shoppers haggling, cries of "Stop, thief!" and stall holders yelling out the bargain prices of their finest quality fruit.

Some stalls only sell one thing and you have to know when to visit them, as they're usually only open one day a week. Other stalls aren't fussy about what they sell. You'll find cabbages and beans alongside cloth and jugs.

All produce is organic, as Roman farmers don't use pesticides. Not because they're eco-friendly – it's just that pesticides haven't been invented yet.

Have a good squeeze to see if the fruit's ripe.

Melons

Choose from juicy melons, ripe apples, and many other delicious fruits.

Grapes

Apples

Ye olde shopping mall

Close to Trajan's forum (see page 48 for a map) you'll find a place known as Trajan's market. But it's more like a shopping mall than a market, with 150 shops and offices around the edges as well as a jumble of stalls in the middle.

You can buy fruit and flowers on the lower levels, with oil, vinegar and exotic imported items higher up.

Don't miss the fifth floor, with its fantastic view, and fishponds where you can buy fish so fresh they're still swimming. (Though I must say, food that's still alive and glaring at me puts me off eating it.)

Farm fresh

A huge variety of produce is brought in daily from farms outside the city.

Don't expect to find potatoes, peppers, tomatoes or chocolate. They come from Central and South America which have no trading links with Rome. In fact, the Romans don't even know America exists.

Jar of honey

Figs

Trajan's market

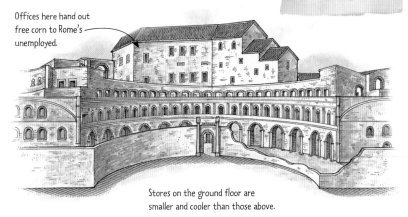

Offices here hand out free corn to Rome's unemployed.

Stores on the ground floor are smaller and cooler than those above.

Consumer watchdogs

The government in Rome can be harsh (what with throwing criminals to the lions) but it does try to protect the little guy sometimes. In order to stop innocent tourists and citizens from being cheated, government officials called *aediles* make regular visits to the markets.

Traders who are caught trying to pull a fast one - by selling rotten fruit or fixing the weighing scales - will face a steep fine.

What's worse than finding a maggot in your apple? How about being fined a large sum for trying to *sell* rotten apples?

66 *The flower stalls are amazing. You can't miss them: they're next to the fish stalls, trying to hide the smell. Buy huge bunches of the cheapest flowers, to freshen up a stuffy apartment.* 99

Someone I met in a forum. I didn't catch his name, but it was good advice.

A steelyard (Roman weighing device)

Some weights are intricately carved, often portraying the heads of famous emperors and generals.

Your goods will probably be weighed on a device called a steelyard, which is a basic weighing scale. Check the merchant isn't leaning on it and trying to trick you when the *aediles* aren't looking.

At the people market

When I first saw a slave auction, I couldn't work out what was going on. I thought it was some kind of mass blind date or perhaps people being picked for a sports team. But then I realized it was an auction, and they were actually selling PEOPLE to the highest bidder.

The slave trade will come as a big culture shock to modern visitors, but Romans think it's as normal as buying and selling olive oil. Many of these slaves are prisoners of war, though poor people occasionally sell their children.

Many slaves get badly treated and have to do hard physical work. But, luckily, not all of them: some of the more educated slaves, especially Greek ones, work as doctors or tutors or librarians. I imagine they have an easier life than many citizens.

Whose are you?

Some slaves wear "identity" tags like this one. But they don't always get to keep their own names. Some have to go by one their master picks for them. It's a dog's life, as a slave.

At auctions, slaves wear signs around their necks advertising their skills, from "Fluent in Greek" to "Very strong." Which is which, do you think?

85

River deliveries

If you want to see where all the goods you've bought enter the city, visit Rome's docks. (See the map below.) Exotic imports arrive here in barges – which is great for Roman shoppers, but I bet the slaves who have to unload it all wish the import business wasn't *quite* so thriving.

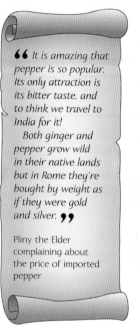

❝ *It is amazing that pepper is so popular. Its only attraction is its bitter taste, and to think we travel to India for it!*

Both ginger and pepper grow wild in their native lands but in Rome they're bought by weight as if they were gold and silver. **❞**

Pliny the Elder complaining about the price of imported pepper

Pons Probus

Pons Aemilius

Pons Fabricius

River Tiber

Warehouses

Insula Tiberina (Tiber Island)

Pons Cestius

The Annona (see right)

Forum Boarium

Theatrum Marcelli

This carving shows a laden barge and is part of a merchant's tomb. Once a merchant, always a merchant, even after death.

These barges come from the sea port of Ostia, 25 km (15 miles) away, where the sea-going merchant ships unload.

Romans trade with countries all over the world – the known world, anyway. There are still vast areas of the Roman world map that are blank, including Australia and America.

Flog your wares

Along the banks of the Tiber, you'll see the gigantic warehouses, or *horrea*, where the barges are unloaded. Some specialize in only one product, such as pepper or spices. You can tell those by the fragrant smells lingering in the air. Others are general storehouses for wine, oil, marble, cloth, timber, wool - well, I could go on all day.

You should be able to find someone here who'll buy the spices you've brought from home. But don't accept the first offer you get - it's always worth haggling.

That's smashing

Keep an eye out for flying pottery as you walk around near the river where the barges are unloading.

Jars for olive oil can't be reused as they're too tricky to clean, so they're smashed and used as ballast to weigh down ships.

Free food

The Annona is the massive state warehouse where free grain for Rome's unemployed is stored and given out. At least a third of Rome's population depends on this food for survival.

But don't be tempted to join the line - visitors passing through town aren't eligible for hand-outs.

Goods in these warehouses are sold to the general public as well as traders.

Hercules

One ancient legend says that the half-god hero Hercules drove a herd of cattle through the Forum Boarium.

A three-headed, fire-breathing monster named Cacus tried to steal some of his cows. But Hercules saw what Cacus was up to and slew him on the spot. (Heroes don't kill monsters, you see, they slay them).

Wholesale markets

I don't imagine you'll be wanting to buy vegetables in bulk, or purchase a herd of cattle. But if you want to have a nose around the places where shopkeepers buy their supplies, visit the Forum Holitorium and the Forum Boarium. (They're right next to the city's docks.) These markets will give you a sense of the vast scale of Roman trade.

The **Forum Holitorium**, which sells fruit and vegetables, lies at the foot of the Capitoline Hill. The **Forum Boarium** is the cattle and poultry market, and it's just beside the Annona. If you want the full trade experience, you could pretend to be a shopkeeper and buy a cow or two. Though I'm not sure how you'd get them home.

Holy cow, look at all those temples! In among the livestock you'll find lots of places of worship.

There are temples to the god of rivers and ports at the cattle market. So you can buy a cow and pray for a safe sea journey at the same time.

88

Part four:
Trips out of Rome

Need a break from the hectic pace of city life? Why not head out of town for a few days? From peaceful fields and picturesque ports, to clifftop walks beside the sea, you'll find plenty of ways to relax.

Of course, you'll need somewhere to stay. If you've made a fortune at the spice markets, you could probably rent yourself a luxury villa, complete with slaves. But if you're starting to run out of cash, try to persuade a wealthy citizen to lend you their place in the country.

Hitching a ride on a cart is a good budget option.

"Giddy up!"

"Thanks!"

Ostia

One interesting spot to visit outside the city is Ostia. As Rome's main seaport, it's always bustling with slaves unloading cargoes, and scribes busily recording every last jar of olive oil. There are officials everywhere, making sure people behave, while merchants hover by the docks, watching over their goods. Think of it like airport customs, minus the sniffer dogs.

A piratical past

Ostia wasn't always the calm, orderly place it is now. In 68BC, it was attacked by pirates. It took thousands of Roman soldiers to fight them off.

These days, you should be safe from pirates in Ostia, but I wouldn't be in a hurry to take a voyage. There are still a few pirates at sea, and shipwrecks are common.

The Romans use lighthouses to navigate at sea. But crashing into rocks is a serious hazard for sailors trying to dock.

Three ports in one

It's far cheaper to send goods by sea than land, so the port does a very brisk trade. With hundreds of ships coming and going, the original port couldn't cope, so two extra docks were built a little way along the coast. Beside one of these, there's a spectacular lighthouse (see the map below.)

But if you're not in a sightseeing mood, you could relax in one of Ostia's many public baths, watch a play, or just stroll around enjoying the sea air.

66 *Everyone who passes scrawls the walls with his graffiti. The only one who's written none is me.* 99

Graffiti on a wall in Ostia

The three docks at Ostia

Dock 2

Lighthouse

Dock 3

Original dock

Ostia

ROME

Tiber

Barges are towed up the Tiber by slaves.

Art at your feet

One of the most popular art forms in Rome is mosaics: pictures made from tiny tiles. In Ostia, look out for some lovely mosaics right under your feet – in the Square of Corporations near the playhouse.

These aren't supposed to be works of art, though. They're actually advertisements for local businesses.

Foreign food

There are over a million people in Rome. That means a lot of hungry mouths to feed – plus some greedy mouths belonging to rich people who see a three-course meal as a snack. The farms around Rome can't keep up, so where does all that food come from?

This is where having an empire comes in handy. The Romans ship in vast amounts of grain from Africa, Egypt and Syria. If you weighed the grain that arrives each year, it would be as heavy as 40,000 elephants.

Boat-spotting

A ship like this one could be carrying thousands of jars of wine, tonnes of timber, or even a cargo of wild, exotic animals.

The massive cargo ships at Ostia are quite a sight to see, with their sails puffed out by the wind. But they're not the fastest vessels, with top speeds of about 7km (about 4 miles) an hour.

It's not surprising it takes three weeks to get to Africa. And that's if the ship isn't wrecked by a storm (or pirates) on the way.

Cargoes unloaded straight onto barges are carried up the Tiber to Rome.

From food to fashion

It's not just grain that arrives at Ostia. There are also ship-loads of everyday stuff such as wool and olive oil, as well as vessels from India laden with spices and gems, and other exotic goods from faraway lands.

Fashion-conscious Romans will be eager to get their hands on a type of purple dye that's shipped in from the land of Phoenicia. (That's Lebanon, in modern times.) The dye is made by "milking" a type of sea snail to extract a purple liquid. This means a) it's very expensive and b) I'm not sure I like purple any more.

Other goods are unloaded onto the quay to be stored in warehouses.

93

This is the life

Top tips for tourists

No. 30: Getting around

If you use enough charm, you might be able to get someone to lend you their carriage for a week. Or you can rent a wagon at the city gates.

I'd allow a few days for your journey, but there are various state-run guesthouses along the way, for overnight stops.

While you're in the city, you may meet someone who invites you to stay, or even offers to lend you their villa (country house) for a week or two. Jump at this chance if you get it.

After the city crowds and grime, you'll think you are in another world. Villas can be magnificent, with landscaped gardens, pools, fountains and statues. As a guest, you'll be allowed - no, expected - to laze around eating and chatting all day.

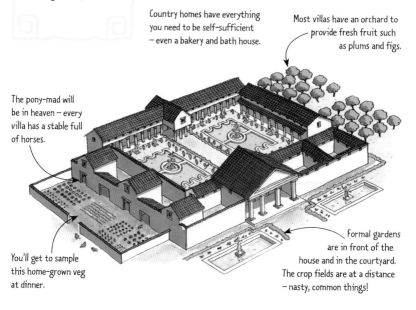

Country homes have everything you need to be self-sufficient – even a bakery and bath house.

Most villas have an orchard to provide fresh fruit such as plums and figs.

The pony-mad will be in heaven – every villa has a stable full of horses.

You'll get to sample this home-grown veg at dinner.

Formal gardens are in front of the house and in the courtyard. The crop fields are at a distance – nasty, common things!

Alright for some

As the guest of a wealthy villa owner, you'll probably have an idyllic break. But not everyone who lives on the estate will be quite so fortunate.

Villas are surrounded by farmland, and the slaves who work there sweat their way through hours and hours of back-breaking toil – from planting crops and clearing up animal dung, to fighting off the wild wolves that come to snack on the plump little pigs on the farm.

Still, if you start feeling guilty about slavery in Rome, you'll never stop.

Health farm

Most villas have bath houses where you can soak yourself whenever you feel like it.

For even more healthy pampering, some villas are just a short trip away from spas that will offer a dip in a smelly but revitalizing mineral bath.

What with that and all the fresh fruit and veg on offer, you'll come back to Rome glowing with health.

Beside the seaside

If your villa is anywhere near the coast, it's worth taking a trip to the sea. Although Romans don't go in for sunbathing, the resorts of Capri and Baiae ("bay-eye") are popular, and their villas are often the last word in luxury. The seas are warm and the beaches are clean – no sewage pipes and no floating plastic bags.

A Roman can look out to sea and think... we own most of the countries out there!

95

Pigs on a Roman country estate have a good life, roaming free. But not usually a long one.

Farm-fresh meat

Country estates often have a pond to provide fresh fish suppers, and the countryside offers a good supply of game, including deer, boar and pheasant.

Many rich Romans hunt for the thrill of the chase, but they pay humble locals to do the more mundane hunting for food.

Oxen are kept for working in the fields. They're the Roman answer to tractors.

Stomping on fruit

If grapes are the main crop at the estate where you're staying, you might get to see wine being made. Though, be warned: seeing the process might put you off the finished product for life.

Once the grapes have been picked, they're trampled on by slaves to get the juice out to make into wine. Yes, that's right. They squish the grapes with their bare feet. I really hope they wash them thoroughly first.

Slaves crushing grapes into mush hold onto poles to keep themselves from slipping.

The grape juice is stored in jars to ferment into wine.

Part five:
Very useful facts

You're already in the know about all kinds of Roman places, customs and quirks.

But before you leave for Rome, here are a few more handy facts. Such as...

• How Romans tell the time

• A little about Roman religion

• What Roman children learn at school

• How Roman money works

• Who's who in Ancient Rome...

...and lots more besides.

Roman children learn Greek poems off by heart.

"O Venus, beauty of the skies, to whom a thousand temples rise..."

Gods, gods, gods

Want a safe sea voyage? Want your party to go with a bang? Then just pick the right god and say a prayer.

There's a god or goddess for almost everything in Rome - from Bacchus, the god of partying, to Neptune, god of the sea.

Blessed be the emperor

Roman religion has two basic branches to it - state religion and private religion.

The first kind is run by professional priests and priestesses who perform elaborate rituals. It focuses on worshipping official Roman gods and also dead emperors, who are seen as gods too.

But Romans are very wary about offending foreign gods, so they often add the deities of conquered enemies to the (increasingly long) official list, just to be on the safe side.

Ceremonies take place outside the temple. All those people couldn't possibly fit inside.

98

Gods & goddesses

Here are a few of the "official" state gods:

Jupiter: King of the gods. Tends to throw thunderbolts when grumpy. His wife, Juno, is goddess of women and marriage and has a temper almost as bad as her husband's.

A statue of Jupiter. He's the boss. Do not make him angry.

Minerva: Goddess of war and wisdom. Clever, resourceful, has a pet owl - but no relation to a certain boy wizard.

Mars: God of war. Must like the Romans, considering how many fights they win.

Venus: Goddess of love. Goes out with Mars but married to another god - the gods' lives are one big soap opera.

This is Jupiter's wife Juno. Don't make her angry either.

Mercury: God of thieves and trade.

Private religion

Each household has its own spirits (*lares*) to protect them, like friendly poltergeists. The family prays to them and offers gifts of fruit and wine. There are lots of other types of spirits, too, including spirits who guard the kitchen storeroom, called *penates*. (So it's their fault if the meat goes bad.)

The god of thieves and trade, Mercury, is also Jupiter's messenger.

99

With so many festivals, I do wonder how Romans find time to conquer people.

Calendar of festivals

There are over 200 religious festivals each year in Rome. There's only room to list a few of them here, but your trip is bound to coincide with at least one. If one of these particularly appeals, you could try to plan your trip around it.

15 February - Lupercalia

At a cave on the Palatine Hill, two teams put on goatskins and race around the hill. The racers also carry whips and give people they pass a (gentle) swishing. Being hit by these is supposed to make childbirth easier, so women will get in the way on purpose.

15 March - Anna Perenna

Take a picnic to the Tiber - with plenty to drink. Romans believe the more they drink on this day, the longer they'll live - hmm, not the best health advice I've ever heard.

21 April - Parilia

Bake a cake and light some candles - it's Rome's official birthday! Actually, I don't think birthday cakes or candles have been invented yet, but Romans organize a massive celebration for the "birth" of Rome, including bonfires and large outdoor feasts.

28 April - Ludi Florales

A carnival for Flora, goddess of flowers. So, one to avoid if you get hay fever. There are special, spring-like games with gladiators hunting hares and goats. Not exactly a fair fight - burly armed gladiator vs. billy goat.

Romans don't need an excuse for a feast, but during Parilia, even poor people get to join in.

9 June - Vestalia

A festival for the goddess Vesta. Note: the bakeries will be shut, but the Vestal Virgins (who worship Vesta) take over baking duties.

At the Ludi Romani, you can party with gods. But don't expect divine wisdom – they're only statues.

12 August - Feast of Mercury

A massive - free - public feast. It's funded by a tax that businessmen pay on their profits each year. Tuck in!

5-9 September - Ludi Romani

A festival of Games, races and plays. If you're at the grand banquet, some guests might seem rather quiet - statues of gods are dressed and laid on couches to join in.

17 December - Saturnalia

A topsy-turvy time, when slaves play at being master and the masters serve them. Slaves still do the cooking though. Can't have the world going *completely* crazy.

Top tips for tourists

No. 31: Dress down day

During Saturnalia, you don't have to wear a *toga* to fit in with even the most upper-crust Romans. So relax and enjoy the party without having to worry about keeping all that heavy material draped around you.

Most men wear belts, but gold buckles like this are a fashion statement. That statement is, "I'm rich!"

This gold ring has a hand-carved gemstone – yet another status symbol.

What to wear

When you travel to Ancient Rome, you'll need to decide what kind of Roman you're pretending to be, and dress appropriately.

If you want to be invited to the best parties, then dress to impress. For men, that means wearing a *toga* - a garment made from a large rectangle of cloth. Wealthy women wear dresses and lots of jewels.

Steer clear of a purple-striped *toga*: only a select few - mostly senators and their wives - are allowed to wear purple. Faking it as a citizen is one thing, but pretending to be a senator is not a good idea, unless you're incredibly good at disguises. Most senators are famous faces around town.

Fabrics to dye for

Clothes tend to be made of wool or linen, but if you want to splash out, you could get a (hideously expensive) cloak made from imported linen or silk. Warning: this might mean you're eating nothing but bread for the rest of your trip.

Men tend to wear clothes in natural, undyed shades, but women dye theirs with natural vegetable and mineral dyes.

Suits you, sir

Only Roman citizens and their sons are allowed to wear *togas*. If you're not a citizen, you'd sometimes wear a cloak outside. As underwear, men usually wear a loincloth (no boxer shorts) which they generally keep on at night. Over this, they wear a simple tunic.

Younger men wear short tunics.

Older men wear longer tunics. The purple stripe shows that the wearer is a senator.

Togas are very heavy, not to mention tricky to wear. You try walking around while trying to keep huge swathes of cloth over a shoulder.

But don't be tempted to leave your *toga* at home, unless you want to be mistaken for a slave or some other riff-raff. Remember, you are a Roman citizen. Wear your toga with pride – and more than a smidgeon of arrogance.

Putting on a *toga*

1. Drape over the left shoulder first.

2. Bring the other end in front of you.

3. Throw it over your left shoulder.

4. Tuck a section into your belt.

A *stola*

The *palla* is a large shawl, worn wrapped around the body and head and then thrown over one shoulder.

Magical necklaces

When a Roman child is born, he or she is given a locket or *bulla*. It's stuffed with magic charms to protect the child from evil spirits and other harmful forces. (Romans believe that a lot of things are out to get them.)

Women's fashions

To modern eyes, a typical Roman woman's outfit will probably look like a nightdress and a sheet. You can't just slip on a dress and go - there's a lot of faffing and fiddling around with drapey fabric.

Female underclothes are actually more or less the same as the ones men wear - a few scraps of fabric as a loincloth, then a tunic over the top. Over that goes a long dress called a *stola*. Wealthier women wear silk ones in dazzling colours including red, yellow, green and blue. Dressier *stolas*, with elaborate embroidery, are worn to parties and important public functions.

On top of the *stola*, many women wear a palla, a long, rectangular scarf. When out and about, they cover their heads with their *palla* or a veil - nice girls don't show their face and hair to all and sundry.

Children

Very young children run around in short, simple tunics. But, from an early age, the sons of citizens wear a mini *toga*, called a *toga praetexta*, and girls a *stola*. There's no escaping fiddly clothing, even as a kid.

A whiter shade of pale

Tans aren't trendy in Rome and pale skin is THE look for the fashionable set, so arms and faces are whitened with powdered chalk. Sometimes they use lead, too, which can kill you. (You'd definitely be pale then.)

Ash is used to darken eyelids and brows; lips and cheeks are reddened with plant dye or red wine. Cosmetics can smell terrible, so be generous with your perfume, to cover up the symphony of strange odours.

> Top tips
> for tourists
>
> No. 33: Why dye?
>
> Blonde and red hair are all the rage in Rome, but you don't need to dye your hair to follow fashion. Why not just buy a wig made from the hair of a blonde or red-haired slave?

Hair-raising experiences

Rich women have to suffer hours of having their hair tugged around and messed with. They usually wear their hair piled high and teased into ringlets or braids.

Men get off more lightly, as most sport a close crop. But they still have to face the daily torture of a visit to the barber for a shave. In a time of very basic razors and no shaving foam... well, let's just say that a freshly-shaven man in Rome runs the risk of looking like he's just been attacked by an angry cat.

Getting a shave in Rome means a world of pain. Luckily, beards are becoming more fashionable.

Education

You're in Rome (I assume) to enjoy yourself, not go to school. But knowing how children are educated here will help you get inside the Roman mind.

As with everything here, there's a sharp divide between rich and poor. Poor kids don't go to school, as they need to start earning money as soon as possible. Very rich kids have private tutors, while other, not-quite-so-rich-but-still-well-to-do children go to school (or *ludus*) from ages 6-11.

Hard work before lunch

A family slave called a *pedagogus* takes children to and from school.

The school day runs from dawn until noon without a break, which is pretty hard work for the little ones. There's no playing around or fingerpainting either. Romans learn to be serious from an early age.

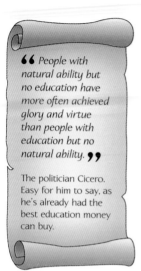

This slave will keep an eye on the kids while they're at school, too.

What do they learn?

Lessons cover the basics: reading, writing and arithmetic. The methods are basic, too, and one of the most common chores is to recite from memory - none of that modern "learning is fun" nonsense.

Arithmetic is equally low-tech. It's taught using fingers and an *abacus* - the ancient version of a calculator.

Young children recite the alphabet. Older children have to commit tricky literary works to memory.

Unpleasant punishments

Pupils who get questions wrong are in for a hard time. We're not just talking a time-out in the naughty corner here. Teachers are allowed to whip pupils, even just for slipping up. Naughty pupils are given an energetic lashing to "encourage" (read: terrify) them to behave better in future.

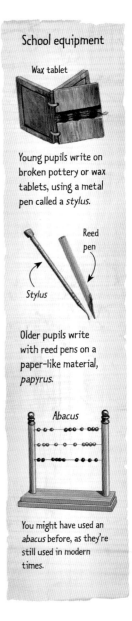

School equipment

Wax tablet

Young pupils write on broken pottery or wax tablets, using a metal pen called a *stylus*.

Reed pen

Stylus

Older pupils write with reed pens on a paper-like material, *papyrus*.

Abacus

You might have used an *abacus* before, as they're still used in modern times.

107

Making paper

Special *papyrus* reeds are cut into strips and soaked in water.

Layers of strips are pressed together and starch is added as glue.

The sheet is beaten with a mallet, left to dry, and polished.

Lots of sheets are stuck together: it's now a scroll.

The cream of the crop

Very few children go on to secondary school. It's only the offspring of the richest Romans who get an education past the age of 11, and even rich girls don't go to school after that. If you're female yourself, try not to appear too knowledgeable while in Rome, or people might get suspicious.

Greek, Greek and more...

...you've guessed it: Greek. If you want to be a success in Rome, you have to be able to quote Greek poetry in your conversation, whether you're talking about gardening, or the meaning of life. So, while children study everything from geography and mythology to astronomy and mathematics, a lot of the day is spent studying Greek poems. Pupils have to learn these off by heart, then spout them on demand. Dull? Maybe. But it avoids a lifetime of looking stupid at parties.

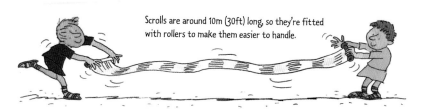

Scrolls are around 10m (30ft) long, so they're fitted with rollers to make them easier to handle.

Learning to argue

Public speaking is a vital skill for anyone who wants to go into law or politics - and that's almost everyone from a "good" family in Rome. From about 13, rich boys are taught the tricky art of making speeches by a teacher known as a *rhetor*.

They're taught how to write speeches, using various exercises; for example, trying to say the same thing a dozen different ways. The *rhetor* also dreams up bizarre scenarios for his pupils to debate, such as: "Imagine you've been shipwrecked. Why do you have more right to claim the goods that have been washed up than the other survivors?" Or they might have to write a speech from the point of view of an ape.

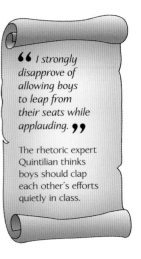

❝ *I strongly disapprove of allowing boys to leap from their seats while applauding.* **❞**

The rhetoric expert Quintilian thinks boys should clap each other's efforts quietly in class.

Getting ready to rule

All this training is to help upper class boys take their place as citizens and future rulers of the empire. Roman politics is a dog-eat-dog world, so they'll need their wits about them - not just to get ahead, but to stay alive. Being good at dropping and picking up on hints is vital, in a world where everyone's plotting against everyone else.

Training can last for years, with the luckiest being sent to Greece to finish their education.

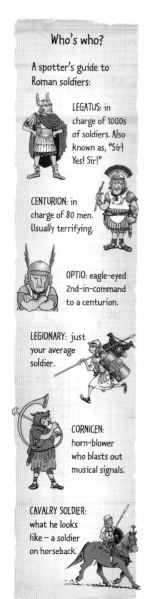

Who's who?

A spotter's guide to Roman soldiers:

LEGATUS: in charge of 1000s of soldiers. Also known as, "Sir! Yes! Sir!"

CENTURION: in charge of 80 men. Usually terrifying.

OPTIO: eagle-eyed 2nd-in-command to a centurion.

LEGIONARY: just your average soldier.

CORNICEN: horn-blower who blasts out musical signals.

CAVALRY SOLDIER: what he looks like – a soldier on horseback.

Death or glory

Without its crack army troops, Rome would be just another city. And the Roman army is not only well trained and armed to the teeth – years of real-life, blood-and-guts experience on the battlefield have turned it into a lean, mean invading machine.

BYO weapons

In the old days, the army wasn't a professional outfit. It was made up of farmers armed with home-made weapons. But as Rome got richer, the army turned pro. Soldiers started getting paid and were given a uniform, weapons and training.

A hard life

But though soldiers are paid and well supplied, it's far from an easy life. Troublemakers have their rations cut, and if you make one stupid mistake, you get flogged. Plus, if a group of soldiers mutinies, every tenth man is executed. This is the origin of the term "to decimate" – to reduce by 1/10th. Many modern adults get this wrong – try testing a few at home.

110

Pitching camp

At the end of a long day's march, soldiers have to build their own overnight camp. These go up quickly and always look similar.

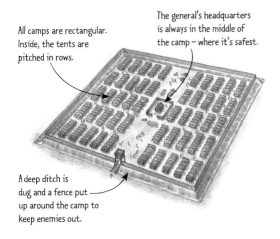

The general's headquarters is always in the middle of the camp – where it's safest.

All camps are rectangular. Inside, the tents are pitched in rows.

A deep ditch is dug and a fence put up around the camp to keep enemies out.

Clever weapons

Standard weapons issue includes: a short stabbing sword, 60cm (2ft) long, hung from the right side of the belt; a dagger, hung from the left; and two *pila* (javelins), one heavy, one light. These have wooden shafts with a middle section of soft iron, deliberately designed to bend as the spear hits its target. This is to prevent the enemy from throwing them back.

Top tips for tourists

No. 34: Marching orders

If you see an army on the march, try to catch some of the orders being yelled at them....

AD SIGNA – Fall in!
INTENTE – Atten-shun!
LAXATE – Stand at ease
PROCEDITE – Forward!

A cooking pot is just one of the many items in a soldier's pack. And it won't be the heaviest.

A sword *(gladius)* – one in a decorated scabbard like this would belong to a *legatus* or someone of a fairly high rank.

111

Legionaries like this one helped make Rome great. (And helped make Rome's enemies dead.)

How many soldiers?

A *contubernium*: 8 men who share a tent and (in theory) look out for each other in battle.

10 *contubernia* make up 1 century of 80 men.

Centuries group together into cohorts. Each legion = 10 cohorts. Any other questions, ask a soldier in a tavern. But ask nicely. They're armed.

Free uniform (sort of)

Every soldier is given a uniform but the cost is taken out of his pay. The uniform usually includes a wool or linen tunic, and a cloak, plus breeches if you're posted somewhere chilly.

Over that, there's chain mail or a leather tunic with metal strips. These are impressively tough, but they don't cover your limbs: one sneaky stab and you'd be helpless on the floor, clutching your leg.

Soldiers generally wear sandals, except on a long march, when they change into boots.

To keep his head safe and in one piece, every soldier gets a solid metal helmet.

A well-oiled machine

The army is grouped into eight "legions" of 5,000 men. Each of these is broken down into smaller groups, so each and every soldier in the Roman army knows his place in the pecking order - who to obey and who to boss around.

112

Legions and hangers-on

As well as soldiers, legions contain doctors, clerks, priests, engineers and servants. Each camp feels like a mini city. They also have *auxiliaries* – provincial non-citizens – who are usually on horseback. They earn less than *legionaries* (citizen soldiers) and are seen as expendable. Reason no. 94857 why it's better to be a citizen.

Who's who in camp?

Aquilifer: carries the legion's eagle-topped standard into battle, wearing a lion skin over his uniform. He won't find it funny if you go up to him and growl. (Yes, I tried it. No, it wasn't my best idea ever.)

Praefectus castrorum: in charge of building camps. Presumably the one to suck up to if you want the comfiest place to sleep.

Signifer: carries the century's standard and organizes soldiers' funerals. This job tends to attract serious, straight-faced types.

Tesserarius: the army spy, who gives the soldiers their password for the day. He's not quite as glam as James Bond, though.

Top tips
for tourists

No. 35: Hadrian's guards

The soldiers you're most likely to run into in Rome are the Praetorian Guard. These are the emperor's personal bodyguards, and they have spies all over the city. So it's best not to say a bad word against Hadrian, just in case.

A century's standard. All the shiny circles and gold bits are prizes that the century has won in battle. These guys must be good.

A guide to coins

Aureus: made of gold, it's the largest denomination

Denarius: silver -25 *denarii* in an *aureus*

Sestertius: bronze - 4 *sestertii* in a *denarius*

Dupondius: bronze - 2 *dupondii* in a *sestertius*

Semi: bronze -2 *semis* in an *as*

As: copper - 4 *as* in a *sestertius*

Quadrans: copper - 4 *quadrans* in an *as*

Cold hard cash

There's no point bringing 21st century money with you to Rome - you won't be able to exchange it. But if you take my advice and trade spices for coins, you'll have plenty of cash to splash on your trip.

Before you go, it's a good idea to get familiar with what Roman coins look like and what they're worth. In the bustle of a marketplace, you won't have long to check that you've been given the correct change. And Romans don't (usually) give receipts.

Hadrian's lovely head

Before the time of the emperors, various Roman mints each produced their own coins. That got very confusing. But thanks to Emperor Augustus, the monetary system is standardized now and all coins have a fixed value. Watch out for fakes, though. If you're unsure, give a coin a nibble. If it seems suspiciously soft, then don't accept it.

Shiny new coins will have Trajan's or Hadrian's head stamped on them, but if you get a coin with another emperor's head on it, don't worry: you can still use it.

Letters or numbers?

Roman numerals look more like jumbled words than numbers: they're made with various combinations of the letters I, V, X, L, C, D and M.

Four, for example, is written IV, meaning one less than five (V); seven is VII, or five (V) plus two (II). But since all numbers are based around just a few letters, you'll soon be dealing with very long "words". For example, it takes seven letters to write 78:

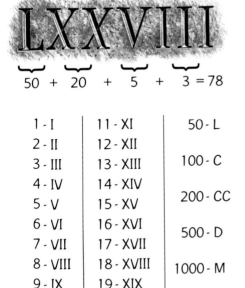

50 + 20 + 5 + 3 = 78

1 - I	11 - XI	50 - L
2 - II	12 - XII	
3 - III	13 - XIII	100 - C
4 - IV	14 - XIV	
5 - V	15 - XV	200 - CC
6 - VI	16 - XVI	
7 - VII	17 - XVII	500 - D
8 - VIII	18 - XVIII	
9 - IX	19 - XIX	1000 - M
10 - X	20 - XX	

Numbers in Latin

1	unus
2	duo
3	tres
4	quattuor
5	quinque
6	sex
7	septem
8	octo
9	novem
10	decem
11	undecem
12	duodecem
50	quinquaginta
100	centum

See page 118 for tips on how to pronounce Latin.

❝ *Money doesn't smell.* **❞**

Emperor Vespasian said this when his son criticized him for taxing public toilets. His point was that coins don't smell, even if you're making money from smelly places.

Laundry

If you have a *toga*, it will need specialist dry-cleaning.

This job – done by someone known as a *fuller* – is not at all pleasant.

First, togas are soaked to clean them.

The chemicals in this bath are bad for the lungs. *Fullers* probably have nasty coughs.

The *togas* are then hung over chemical fires, to bleach them.

They're left to dry, then folded and flattened in a press.

What time is it?

Telling the time in Ancient Rome is a vague business, since there are no clocks - only sundials and water clocks, which aren't very accurate at all. Days last as long as the daylight and the 12 hours of the day aren't divided into minutes. In fact, an hour is longer in summer, when the light lasts longer. So don't expect people to be on time - they don't know what time it is.

Relying on a sundial on a cloudy day is a recipe for disaster.

What year is it?

As a time tourist, you don't want to alert suspicions by asking people what year it is. Plus, it wouldn't help you much, as Romans don't count years the way we do - they count from when Rome was founded, and from the year their emperor began ruling.

What's your name?

Wealthy Romans tend to have three names: a *praenomen* (first name), a *nomen* (family name) – like a surname – and a *cognomen* (another family name and the name that you'd be called by your well-to-do friends).

You'll probably need a name during your stay. So just pick three names from the list on the right, and practise saying, "Yes?" when someone says "your" name.

Top tips for tourists

No. 36: Use an alias

To create a Roman name, just pick a : 1. *praenomen* 2. *nomen* and 3. *cognomen*.

1. Gaius*, Livius, Titus, Sextus, Marcus

2. Claudius*, Antonius, Atius, Didius, Manlius

3. Severus*, Lupus, Gallus

*For girls, take off the "us" and add an "a" to each name.

Newspapers

If you're fluent in Latin, you can grab a daily free paper – in the forum. It's only a page long, all handwritten, so you can get all the latest stories at a glance.

Emergencies

A police and fire-fighting force, the Cohors Vigilum, will come to help if there's a fire, or if you're robbed. Or if you have a really bad day and both happen at once.

Fire is a daily hazard in Rome.

Phrasebook

Handy phrases

Hello	**salve**
Goodbye	**vale**

(Add **domine** (sir) for a man and **domina** (madam) for a woman.)

Yes	**certe**
No	**minime**
Thank you	**gratias ago**
I don't know	**non scio**
I'm sorry	**doleo**
How are you?	**ut vales?**
I'm well	**bene valeo**
Very well	**optime**
Quite well	**satis bene**
Not very well	**non ita bene**
Terrible	**pessime**

Asking directions

Excuse me	**da mihi veniam**
Where is...?	**ubi ... est?**
How do I get to?	**qua via venio ad?**
Straight ahead	**in directum**
Nearby	**in propinquo**
On the left	**a laeva parte** On
the right	**a dextra parte**
Is it far?	**estne longinquum?**

Food and shopping

Bakery	**pistrina**
Butcher	**laniena**
I'm hungry	**esurio**
I would like...	**requiro...**
Milk	**lac**
Eggs	**ova**
Fruit	**pomum**
Vegetables	**holera**
Meat	**caro**
Fish	**piscis**
Bread	**panis**

Pronunciation tips

Pronunciation is easy – for nearly every letter, say it as it is written. Piece of cake.

There are just three exceptions:
'**c**' is pronounced like a '**k**'
'**v**' is pronounced like a '**w**'
'**i**' before a vowel is pronounced like a '**y**'

Examples:
for **panicellus** (bread) say **pani-kellus**
for **novem** (nine) say **no-wem**
for **iam** (now) say **yam**

What's a forum? Useful definitions

aqueduct: a channel for carrying water, often carried on a bridge, which is also called an aqueduct.

basilica: a large public building, in or near the forum, housing law courts, offices and shops. Watch trials here.

citizen: originally, a man born in Rome to Roman parents, who could vote and serve in the army. But, after a while, citizenship was offered to anyone considered worthy. By Hadrian's time, people across the Empire are becoming citizens.

consul: the top government official. Two consuls are elected each year to help run Rome and its armies. They report to the emperor.

domus: a private house, which would be owned by someone wealthy. If you're lucky, you'll get to stay in one of these.

emperor: supreme ruler of all Roman territories. Augustus became the first emperor in 27BC, though he never called himself that.

Empire: (1) all Roman territories; (2) the time when Rome was ruled by emperors, up to the year 476.

forum: an open space in the middle of a Roman town, used for markets, law courts and politics.

hypocaust: central heating – hot air flows through gaps between walls and under floors.

Imperial Rome: the period when Rome was ruled by emperors.

insula: an apartment block – each apartment within the block is called a *cenaculum*.

Republic: a state or country without a king, queen or emperor, whose leaders have been elected into power by the people. Rome was a republic from the 6th century BC until 27BC.

Senate: the group of nobles that governs Rome. By 82BC, there were 600 senators. The Senate's powers are gradually being reduced, as emperors take more power for themselves.

slave: a person with no rights, owned by another. Most slaves are prisoners-of-war.

viaduct: a bridge which carries a road across a river or a valley.

villa: a large house or estate in the country.

Who's who in Ancient Rome

Romans are obsessed with status and pecking order, so here's a handy checklist of who's who in Roman society. That way you'll know who to look up or down to – or sideways at.

Citizens

You already know what a citizen is (right? There's a definition on page 119 if you've forgotten), but here's a little more about the types of citizen you'll run into:

Patricians: the richest citizens. They're the people who make up the ruling class. Senators, consuls and other VIPs will be patricians.

Equites: they're usually businessmen and bankers. Money men who aren't super-upper class, but very comfortable, thank you.

Plebeians: the poorest citizens. If you're undercover as a patrician, don't mingle with them if you can help it. It wouldn't be good for your reputation.

Poets and politicians

When you're chatting to Romans, it's always nice to be able to namedrop celebrated politicians and authors. People will see you as well-informed and in the know.

Also, since you'll be speaking a foreign language, it'll probably be helpful to pick out names you recognize. That way, at least you know who's being talked about, even if you don't know what people are saying about them.

Read on to find out about some of the notable people in Roman history – and, in some cases, in the present – when you're in the year 118 anyway.

Augustus (63BC- the year 14): this great leader was born with the name Octavian, but took the name Augustus when he became ruler. He never called himself an emperor, but he basically was one. The great-nephew of Julius Caesar, he was good at his job, bringing peace and prosperity to Rome.

Caesar, Julius (c.100-44BC): a politician, soldier and writer, who invaded countries all over the place, even as far as Britain. In 46BC, he became the supreme ruler (or "dictator") of Rome. But it was feared he'd make himself king, so he was murdered on March 15 44BC.

Cato (234-149BC): a politician and writer who wrote a famous book about farming.

Catullus (c.84-c.54BC): a poet who wrote love poems and vivid descriptions of Roman life. Like many Romans, he was a fan of all things Greek, and used Greek literary tricks in his poems.

Cicero (106-43BC): a politician, lawyer and writer who was the best public speaker of his day. Roman teachers often quote him.

Domitian (51-96): anyone who opposed this arrogant ruler was murdered, so it's not a surprise that the emperor was eventually assassinated himself.

Hadrian (Born in the year 76, died in the year 138): the emperor in the time you'll be visiting. He's a scholar and soldier who spent lots of time with armies in the provinces, building barriers (including Hadrian's Wall in Britain) against invaders. But, unlike Trajan, the emperor before him, he has no interest in making the Roman empire bigger. It's quite big enough already, thank you.

Horace (65-8BC): a poet, famous for his *Odes*, short poems on topics such as food, wine and the countryside.

Juvenal (c. the year 60-c.130): a poet whose *Satires* criticized the poverty, immorality and injustices of Roman life. Often very rude about people. But he thought they deserved it.

Livy (59BC- the year 17): a historian who wrote a history of Rome and its people. Quote him to show how much you love your "home" – Rome, that is.

Mark Antony (82-30BC): a soldier and politician who was a consul alongside Caesar in 44BC. Mark Antony committed suicide after his defeat by Octavian (*a.k.a.* Augustus) in 30BC.

Martial (c.40-104): a poet who wrote *Epigrams*, a collection of poems about Rome's more lively characters and everyday life in the city. Like Juvenal, he's very sarcastic and rude at times.

Nero (37-68): this emperor was so obsessed with power that he killed anyone who went against him – including his mother. Gossips have claimed he's responsible for a fire in the year 64 which destroyed much of Rome. He killed himself – not because he wanted to, but because his enemies didn't give him any other choice.

Octavian: the emperor Augustus's original name.

Ovid (43BC- the year 18): a poet whose most famous work is *Metamorphoses*, fifteen books of poems on myths and legends. He also gave dating advice in his book the *Ars Amatoria*.

Pliny (c.61-c.113): a writer and lawyer who published the letters he wrote to various famous people.

Plutarch (46-126): author of a set of biographies, called *Lives*, which compare lives and careers of Greek and Roman soldiers and politicians. It's heavy going, but many Shakespeare plays are based on it, so you could always read his versions. That may not sound like a picnic, but compared to *Lives*, Shakespeare is light reading.

Seneca (c.5BC- the year 65): a writer, lawyer and philosopher. Also Nero's tutor. Forced to commit suicide when they fell out.

Suetonius (c.69-140): a historian and government official who wrote about the 12 rulers from Caesar to Domitian.

Tacitus (c.55-c.116): a historian and consul who wrote about the lives of emperors.

Terence (c.195-159BC): a playwright who adapted Greek comedies. Originally a slave, he was freed by his master.

Trajan (c.53-117): a superb general, this emperor made the Empire as large as it would ever be.

Vespasian (9-79): the emperor who restored order after Nero, and began extensive public building works, including the Colosseum.

Virgil (70-19BC): a poet who wrote a poem called *The Aeneid*, which is the story of the history of Rome, as well as being a tragic love story.

Roman emperors

I've already mentioned a few emperors, but here's a list of the important ones. Most of them will be due to rule well after your time in Rome. NB: the very last emperor was Romulus Augustus, who ruled until the year 476. That was when the Roman Empire finally went to pieces. Started by a Romulus, ended by a Romulus.

27BC-the year 14	Augustus
14-37	Tiberius
37-41	Caligula
41-54	Claudius
54-68	Nero
69	Galba; Otho; Vitellius
69-79	Vespasian
79-81	Titus
81-96	Domitian
96-98	Nerva
98-117	Trajan
117-138	Hadrian
138-161	Antoninus Pius
161-180	Marcus Aurelius
180-192	Commodus
193-211	Septimus Severus
211-217	Caracalla
218-222	Elagabalus
222-235	Severus Alexander
270-275	Aurelian
284-305	Diocletian (Eastern part of the empire)
286-305	Maximinian (Western part)
312-337	Constantine
337-361	Constantine's sons
361-364	Julian the Apostate; Jovian
364-379	Valentinian I; Valens; Gratian; Valentinian II
379-392	Theodosius (Eastern part)
395-423	Honorius

Timeline of Ancient Rome

I've scribbled down a few key events in Roman history, in case you're curious.
Remember, the BC dates are counted backwards from the year zero.

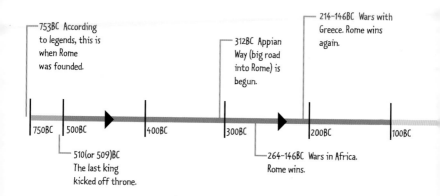

753BC According to legends, this is when Rome was founded.

312BC Appian Way (big road into Rome) is begun.

214–146BC Wars with Greece. Rome wins again.

750BC 500BC 400BC 300BC 200BC 100BC

510(or 509)BC The last king kicked off throne.

264–146BC Wars in Africa. Rome wins.

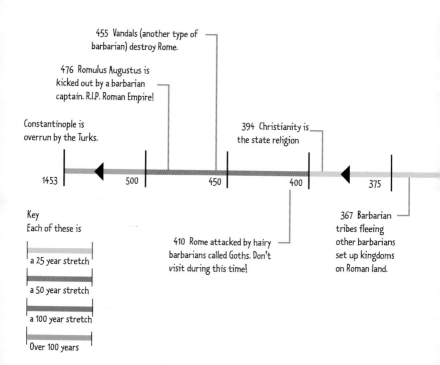

455 Vandals (another type of barbarian) destroy Rome.

476 Romulus Augustus is kicked out by a barbarian captain. R.I.P. Roman Empire!

Constantinople is overrun by the Turks.

394 Christianity is the state religion

1453 500 450 400 375

367 Barbarian tribes fleeing other barbarians set up kingdoms on Roman land.

410 Rome attacked by hairy barbarians called Goths. Don't visit during this time!

Key
Each of these is

a 25 year stretch

a 50 year stretch

a 100 year stretch

Over 100 years

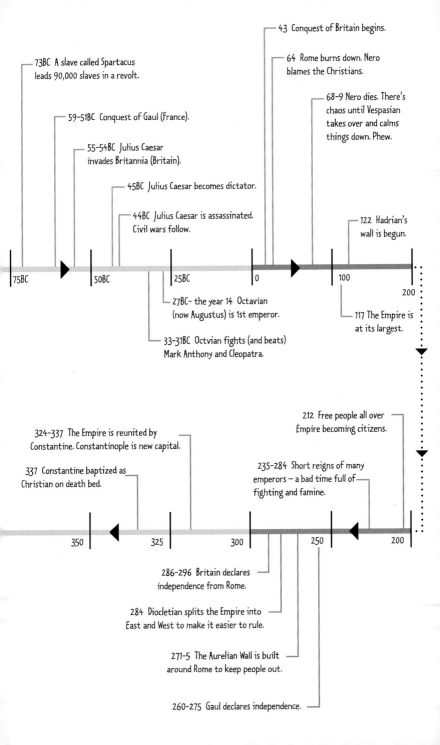

43 Conquest of Britain begins.

73BC A slave called Spartacus leads 90,000 slaves in a revolt.

64 Rome burns down. Nero blames the Christians.

59–51BC Conquest of Gaul (France).

68–9 Nero dies. There's chaos until Vespasian takes over and calms things down. Phew.

55–54BC Julius Caesar invades Britannia (Britain).

45BC Julius Caesar becomes dictator.

44BC Julius Caesar is assassinated. Civil wars follow.

122 Hadrian's wall is begun.

75BC 50BC 25BC 0 100 200

27BC– the year 14 Octavian (now Augustus) is 1st emperor.

117 The Empire is at its largest.

33–31BC Octvian fights (and beats) Mark Anthony and Cleopatra.

212 Free people all over Empire becoming citizens.

324–337 The Empire is reunited by Constantine. Constantinople is new capital.

235–284 Short reigns of many emperors – a bad time full of fighting and famine.

337 Constantine baptized as Christian on death bed.

350 325 300 250 200

286–296 Britain declares independence from Rome.

284 Diocletian splits the Empire into East and West to make it easier to rule.

271–5 The Aurelian Wall is built around Rome to keep people out.

260–275 Gaul declares independence.

Index

Acknowledgements:

Edited by Jane Chisholm

Digital manipulation by Keith Furnival

History consultant: Dr. Anne Millard

Military commands on page 111 taken from the Usborne Roman Soldier's
Handbook and originally provided by the Ermine Street Guard, a
society dedicated to researching the Roman Army.

First published in 2009 by Usborne Publishing Ltd., Usborne House,
83-85 Saffron Hill, London EC1N 8RT, England. www.usborne.com
Copyright © 2009 Usborne Publishing Ltd. The name Usborne and the
devices ♀⊕ are Trade Marks of Usborne Publishing Ltd.

Trajan's Column

Via Lata

6

9

17

CIRCUS FLAMINIUS

11

16

Pons Cestius

RIVER TIBER

Pons Fabricius

TIBER ISLAND

15

14

Map of Ancient Rome

(And some of the sights that you'll read about in this book.)

1 Aqueduct of Nero
2 Baths of Titus
3 Trajan's Baths
4 Subura district
5 Forum Romanum
6 Imperial Fora
7 Colosseum
8 Circus Maximus
9 Pantheon
10 Via Sacra
11 Theatrum Marcelli
12 Arch of Titus
13 Via Appia
14 Rome's docks
15 Forum Boarium
16 Forum Holitorium
17 Theatrum Pompei
18 Arch of Augustus

Vicus Tuscus

TO THE PORT OF OSTIA